flower Girlies

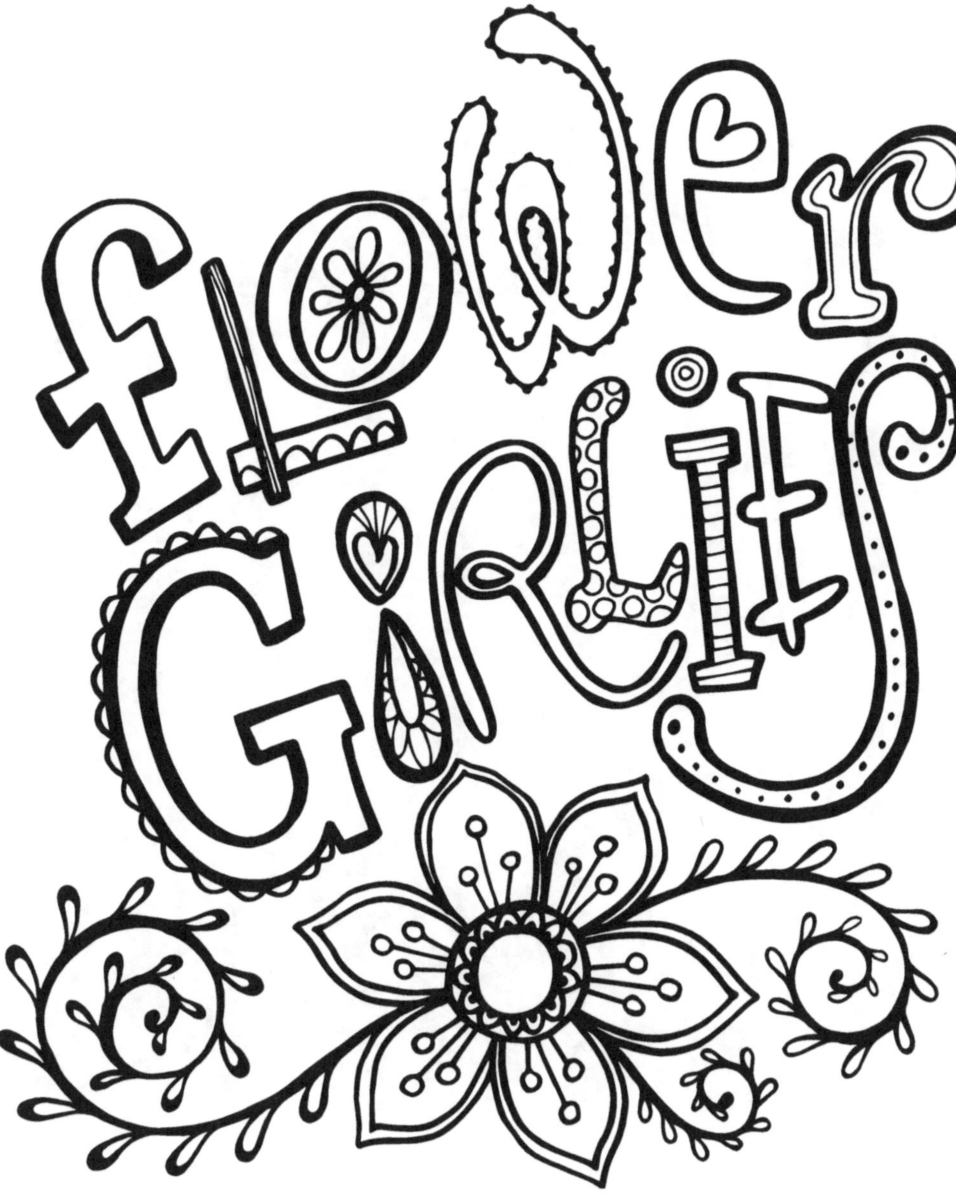

A COLORING BOOK BY

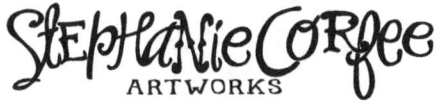

Stephanie Corfee
ARTWORKS

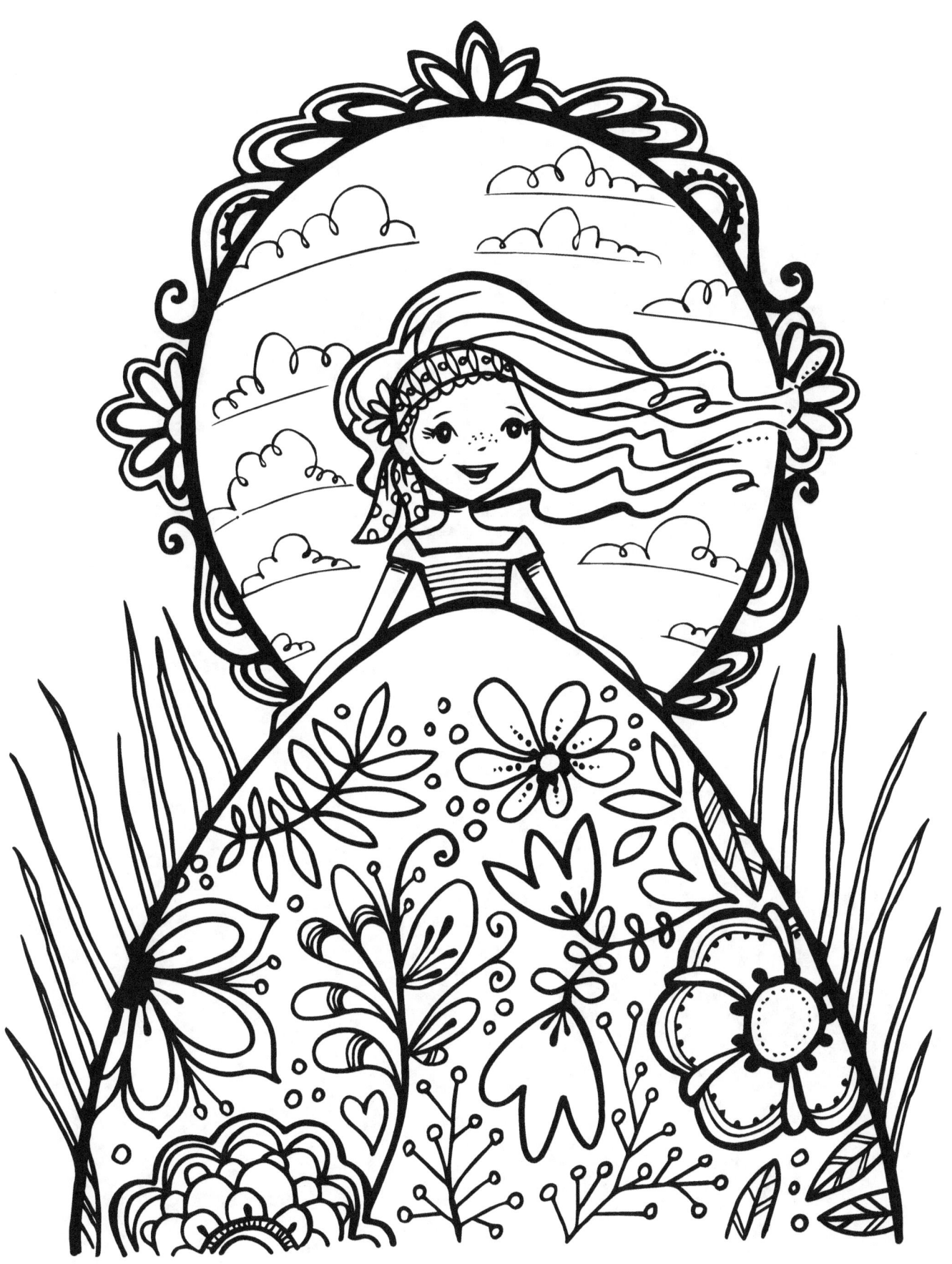

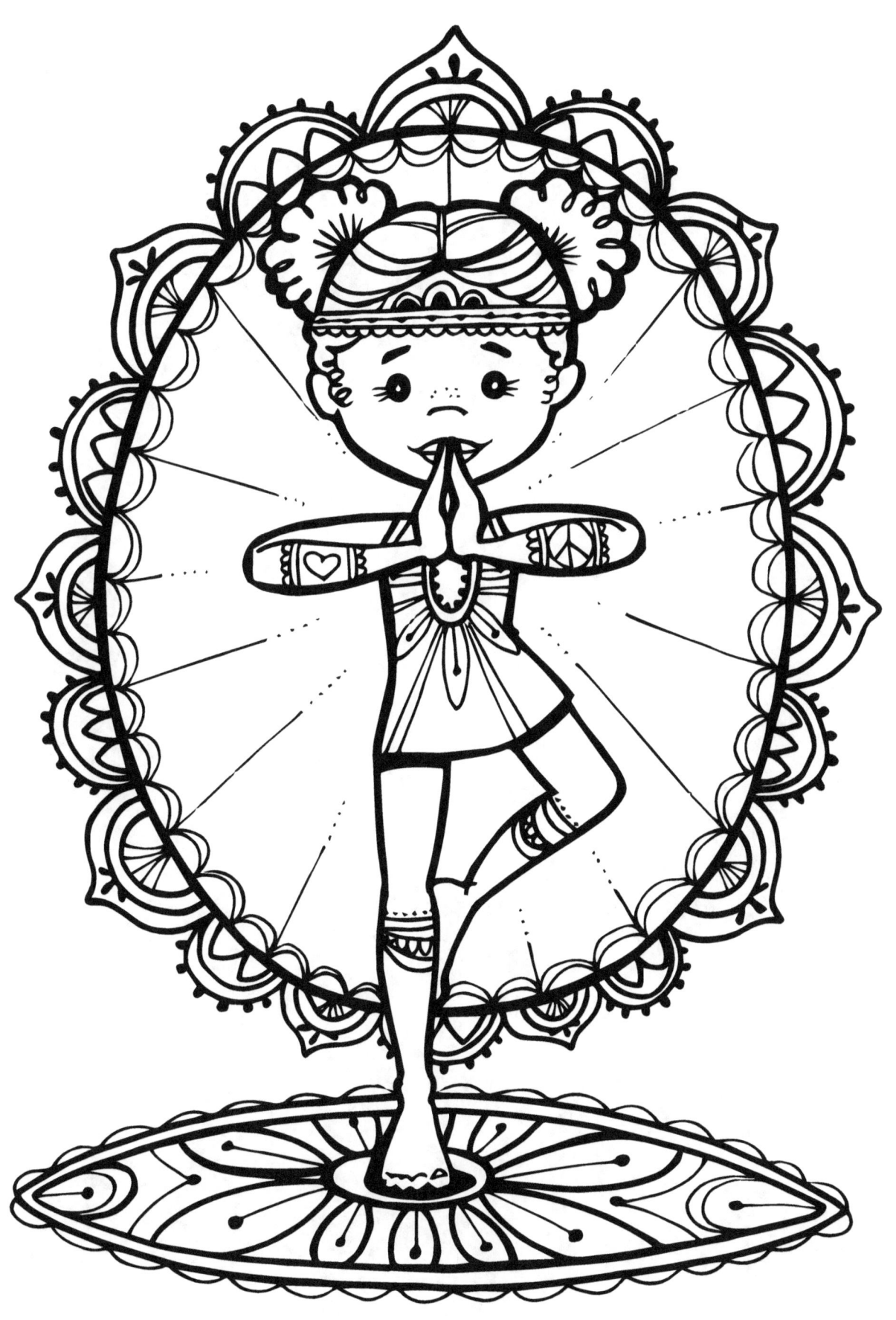

flower girlies

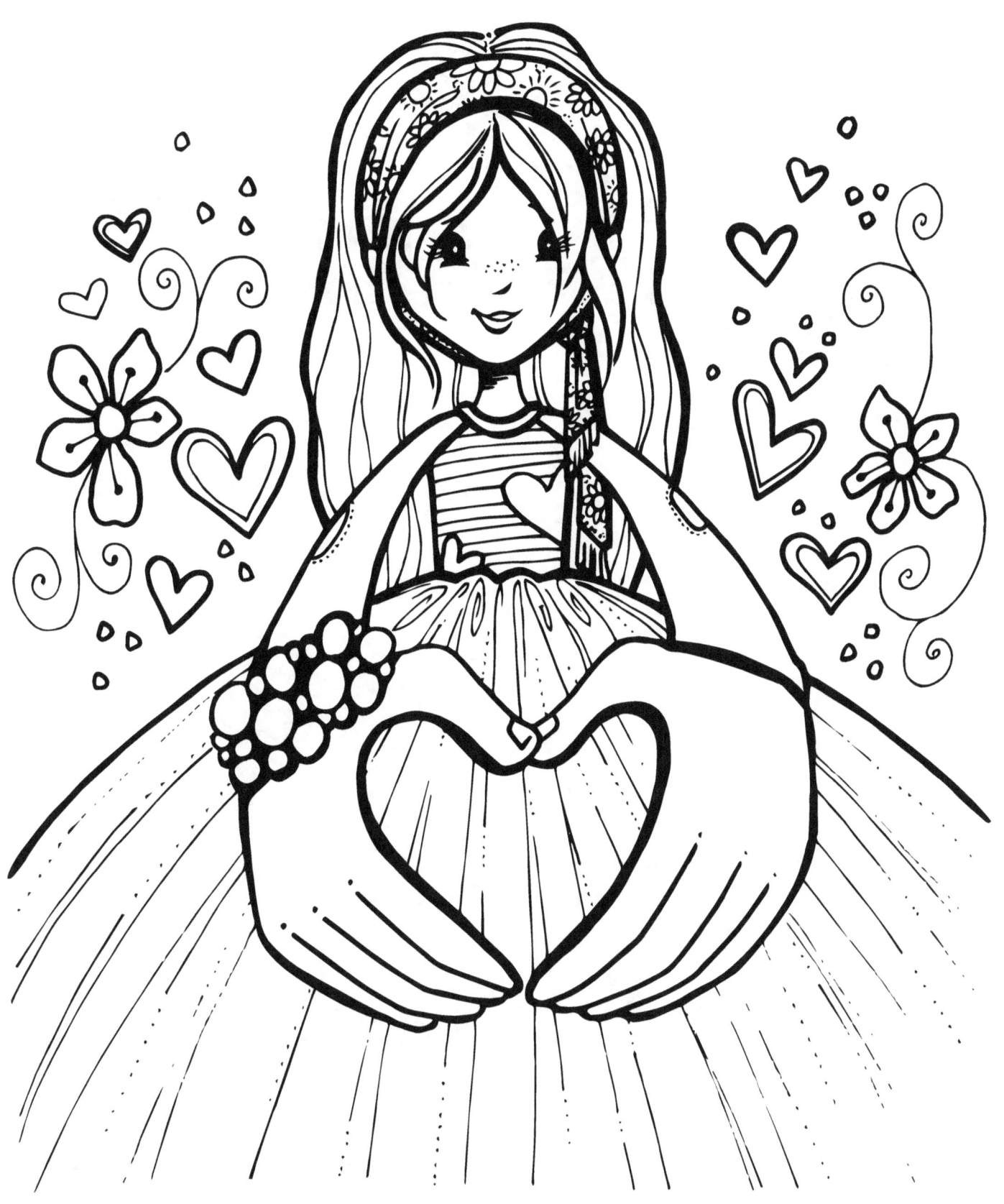

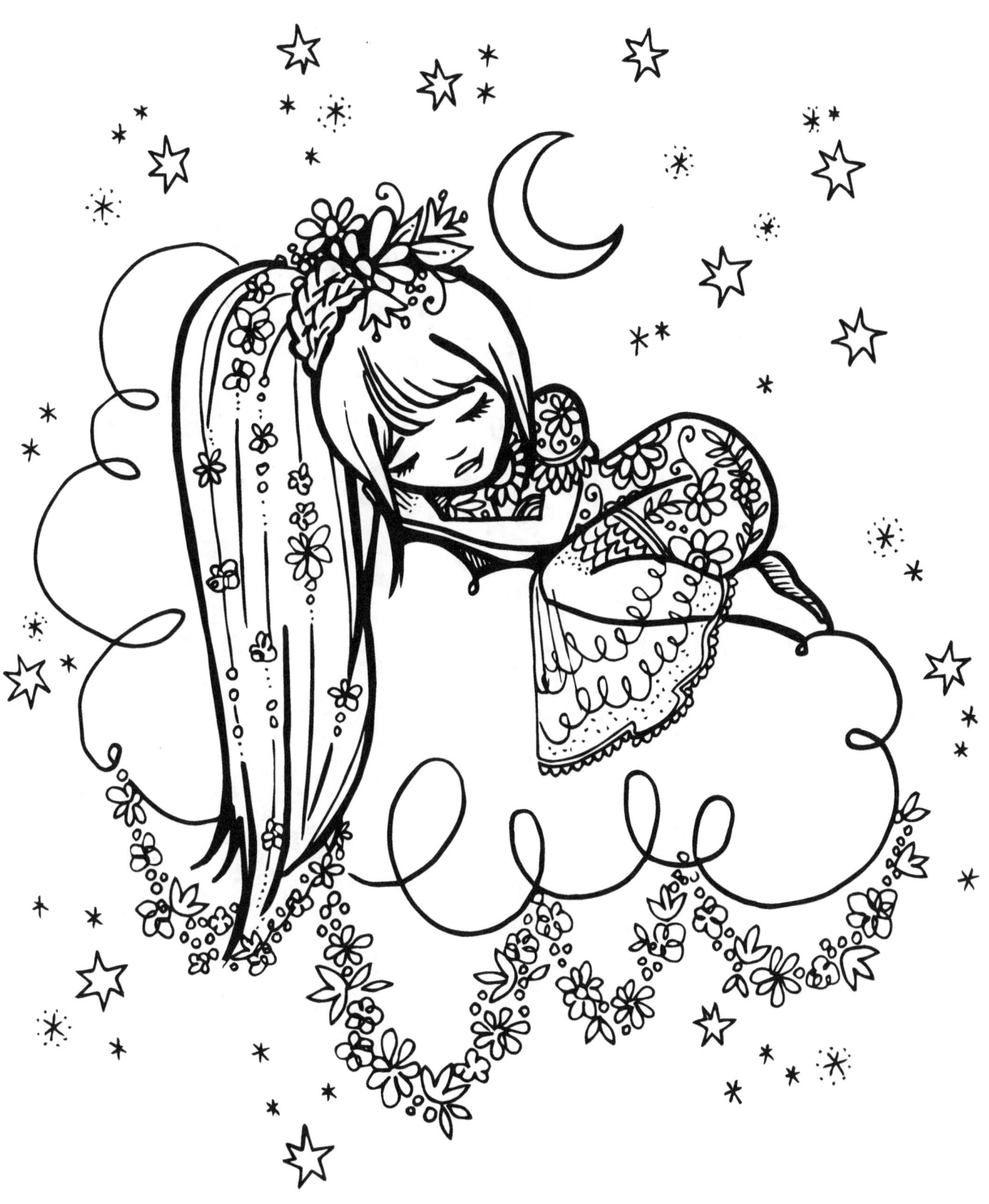

flower girlies

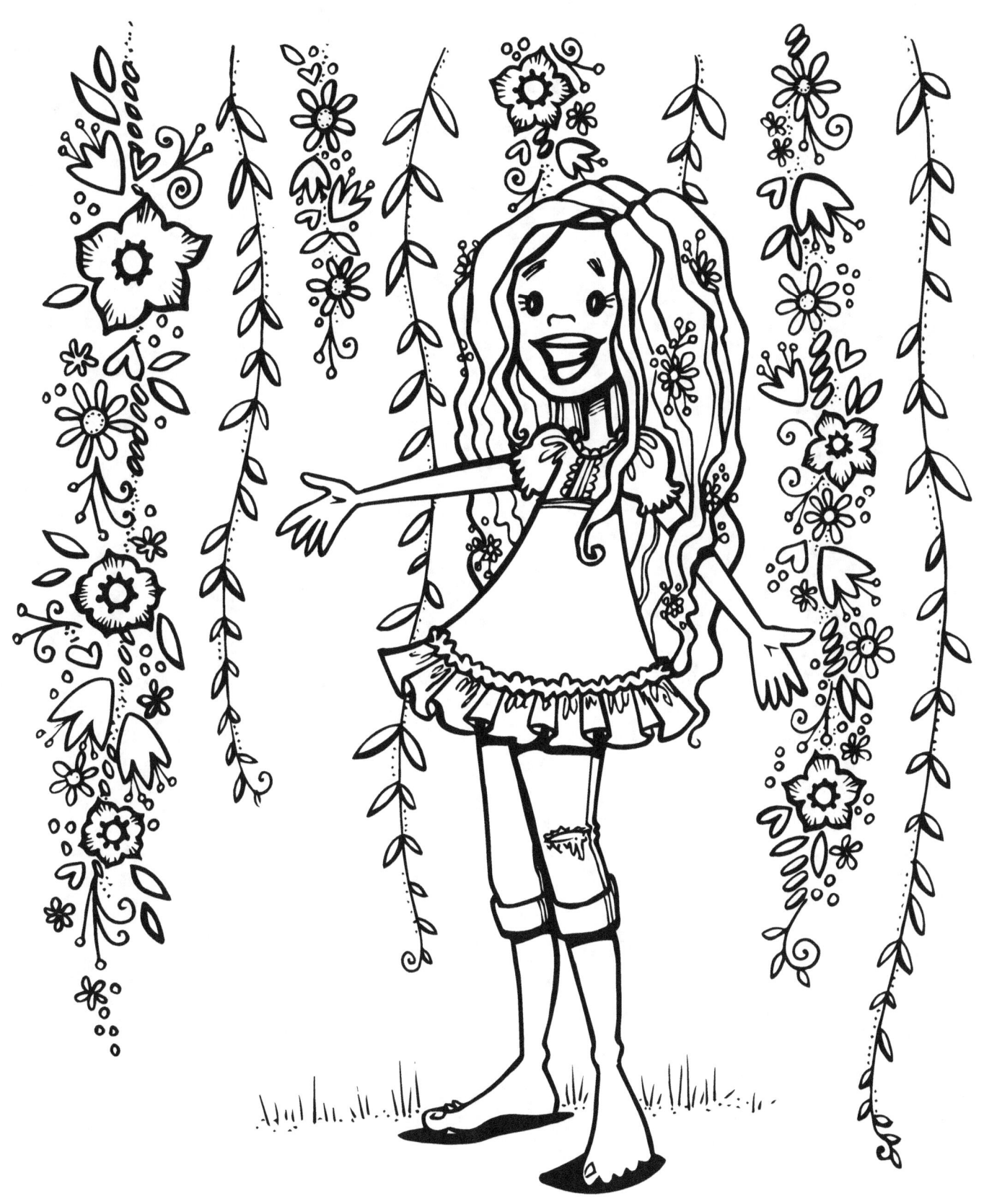

flower girlies

StephanieCorfee
ARTWORKS

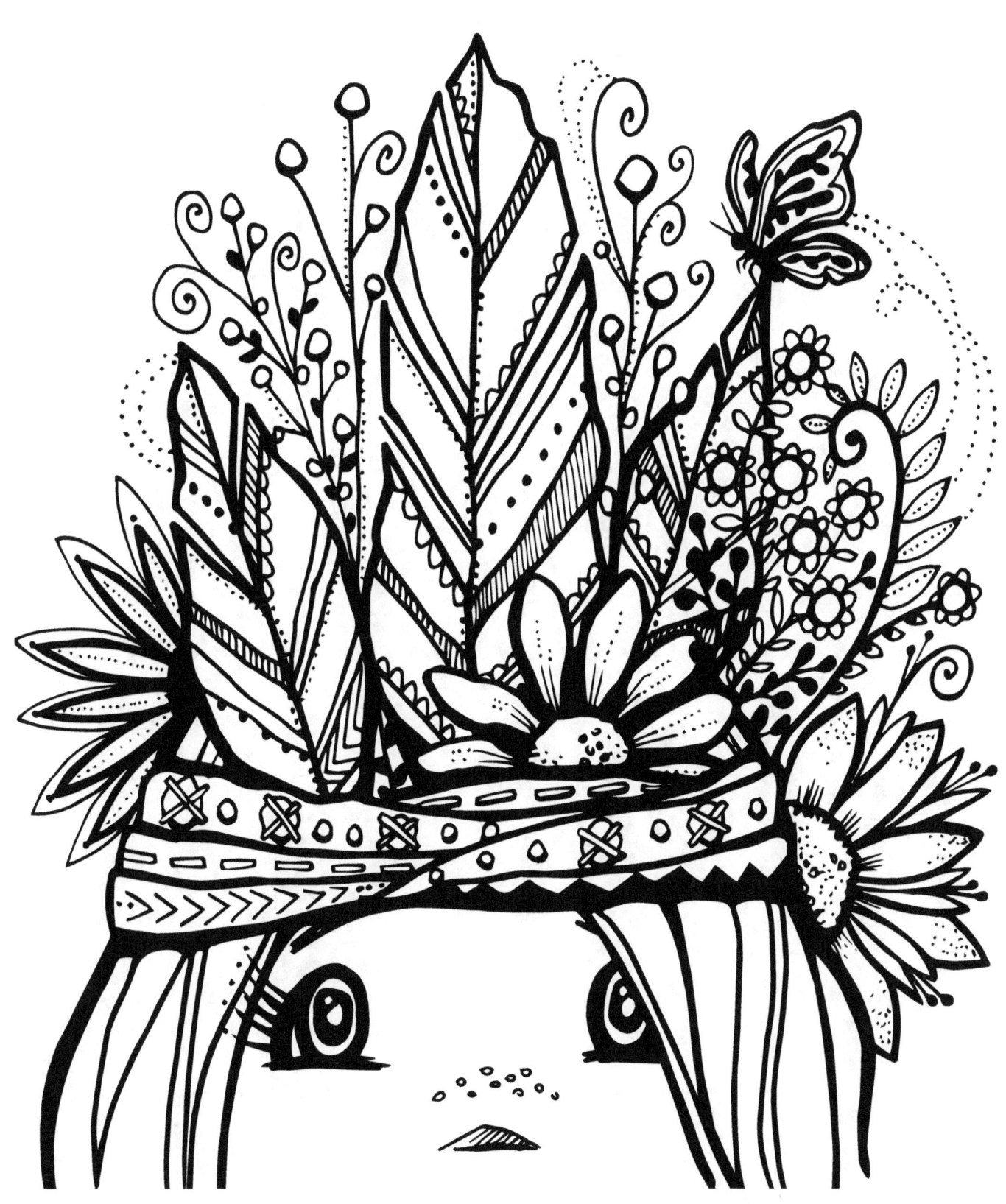

flower girlies

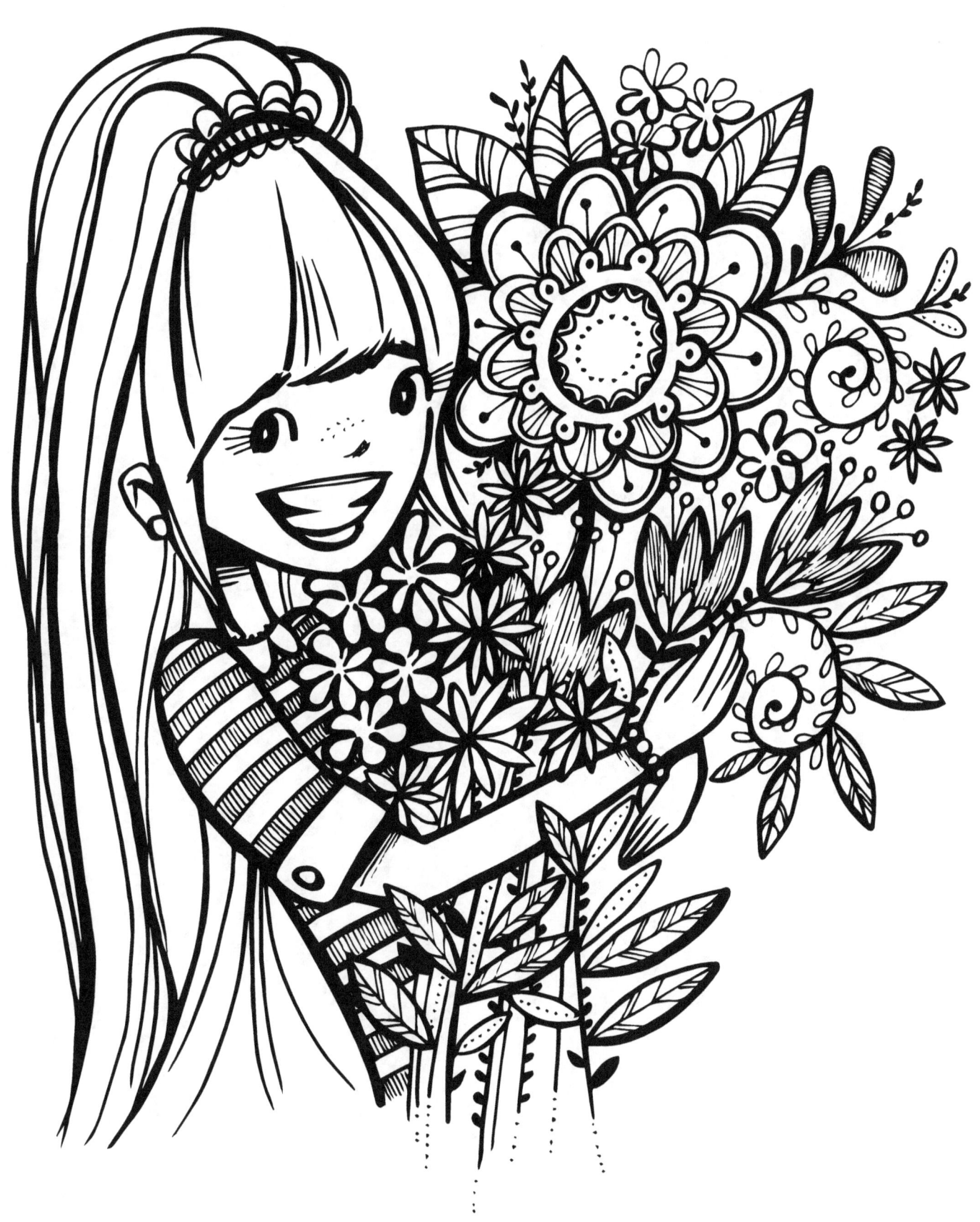

flower girlies

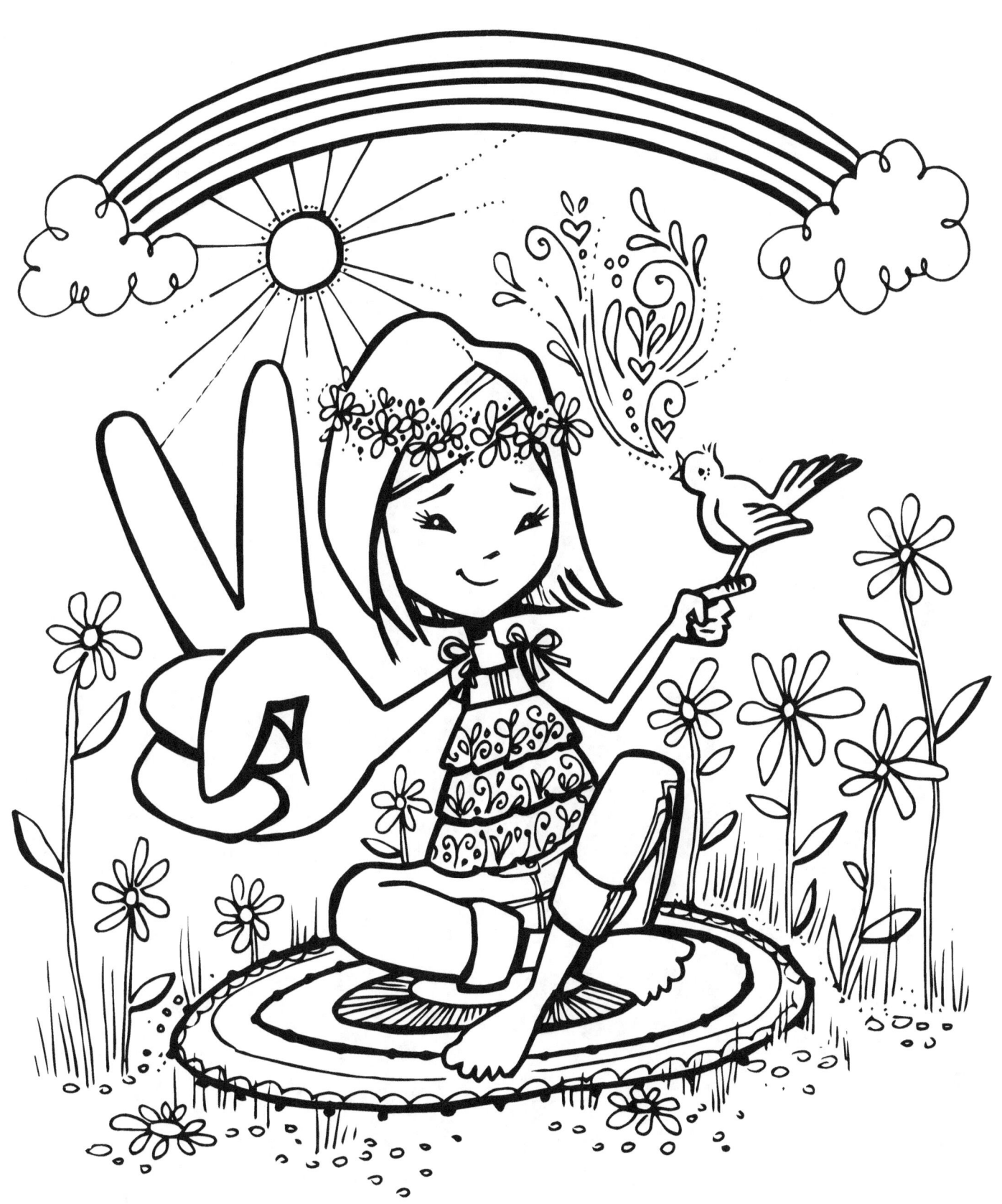

flower girlies

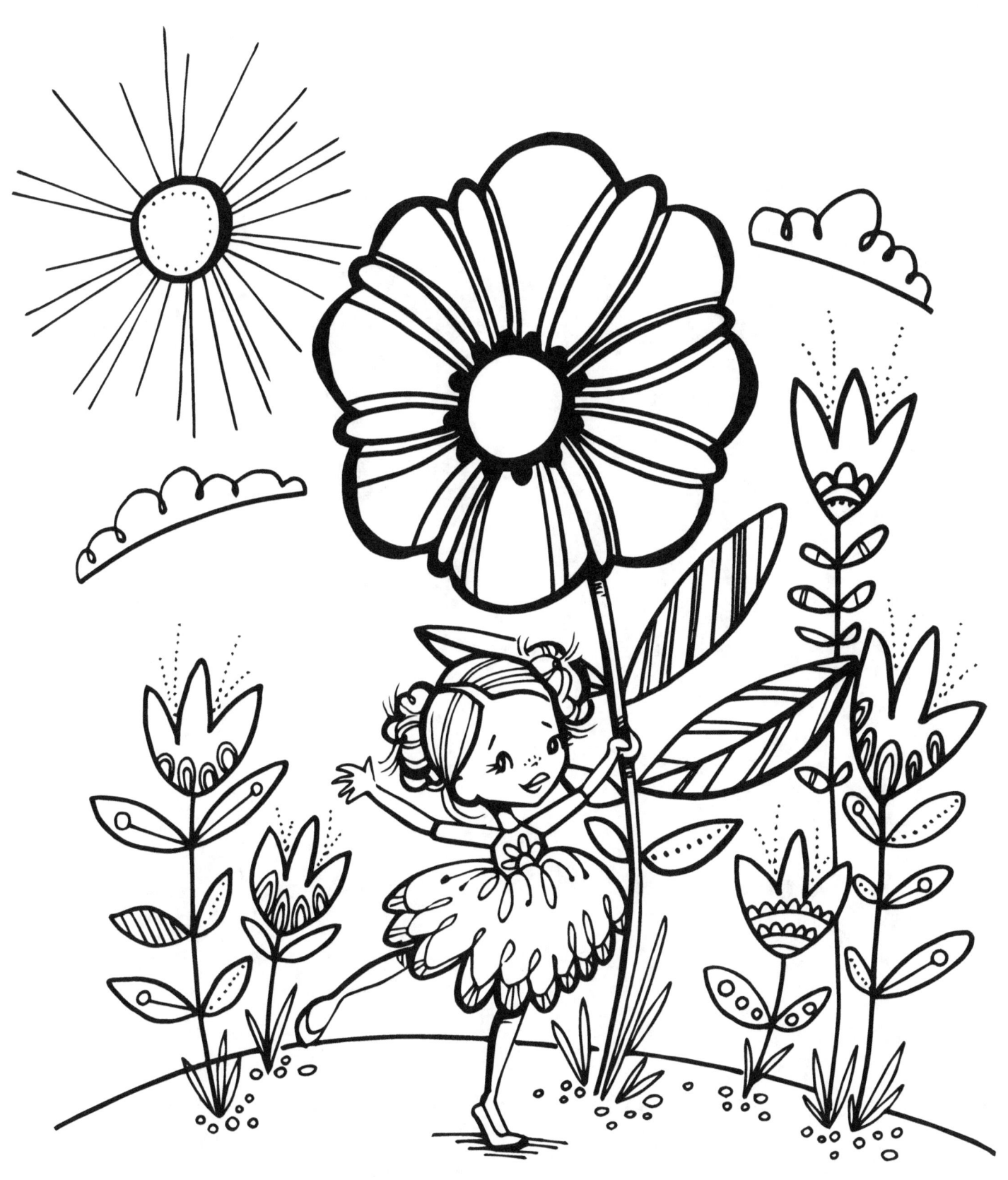

flower girlies

Stephanie Corfee
ARTWORKS

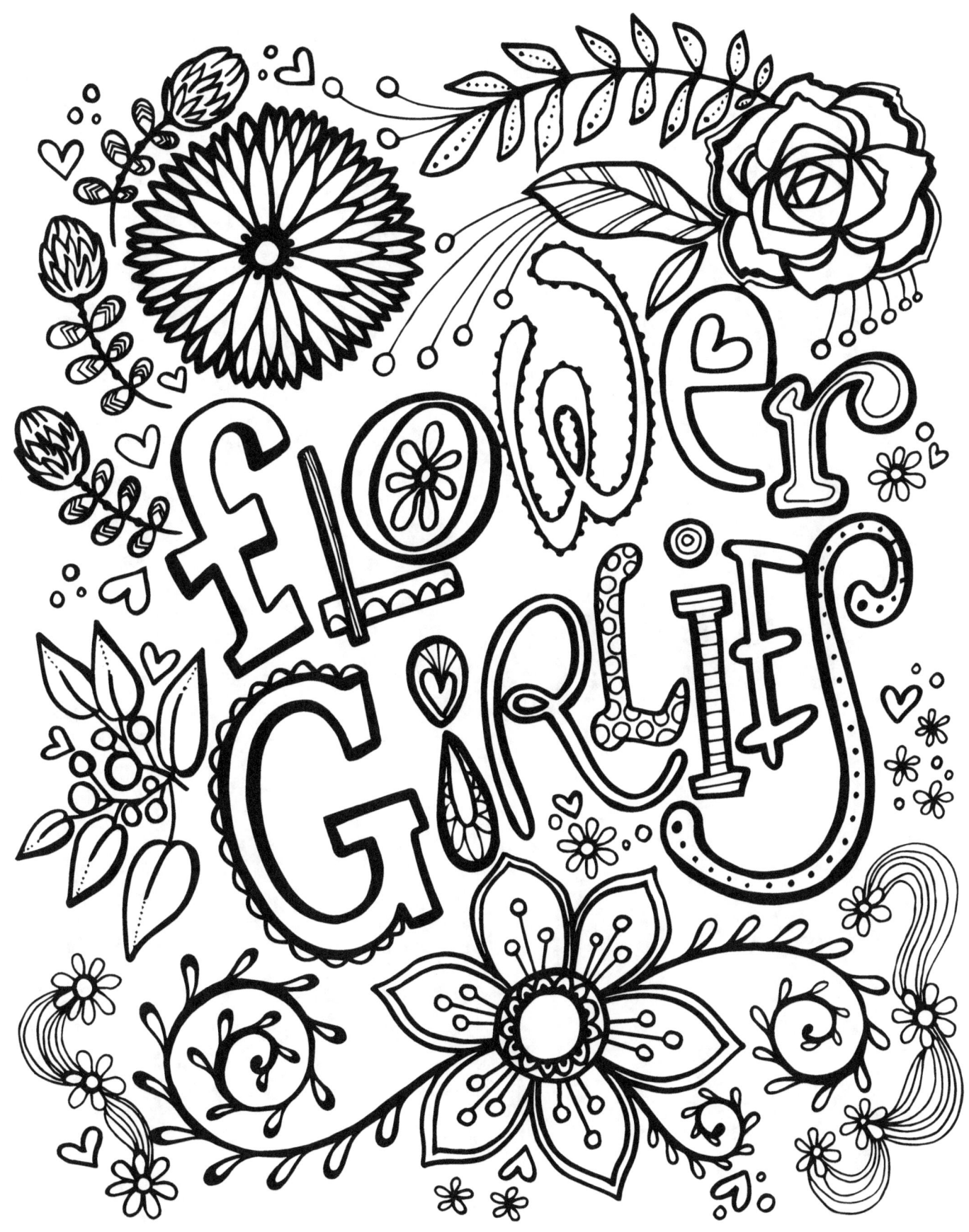

flower girlies

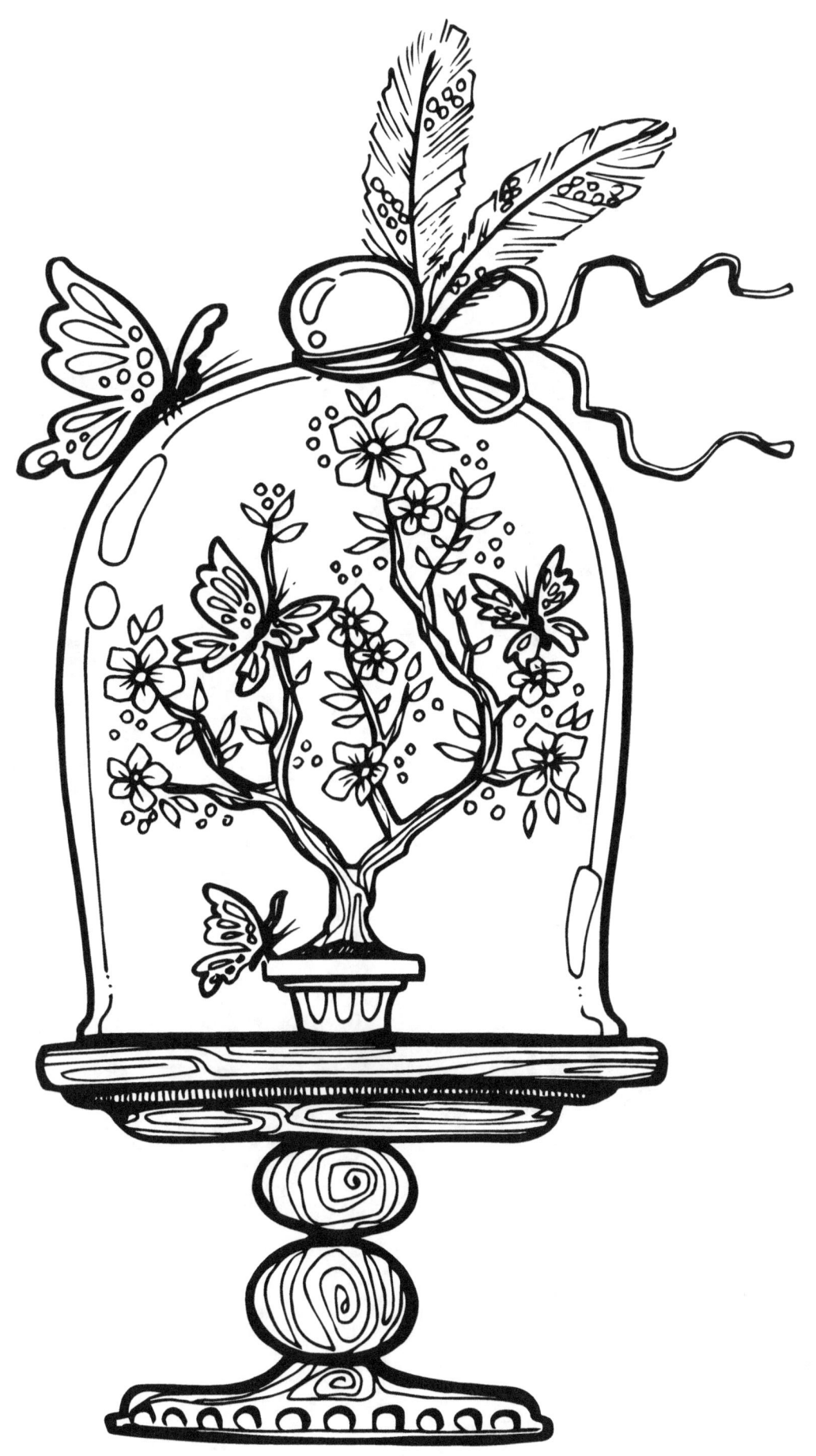

flower girlies

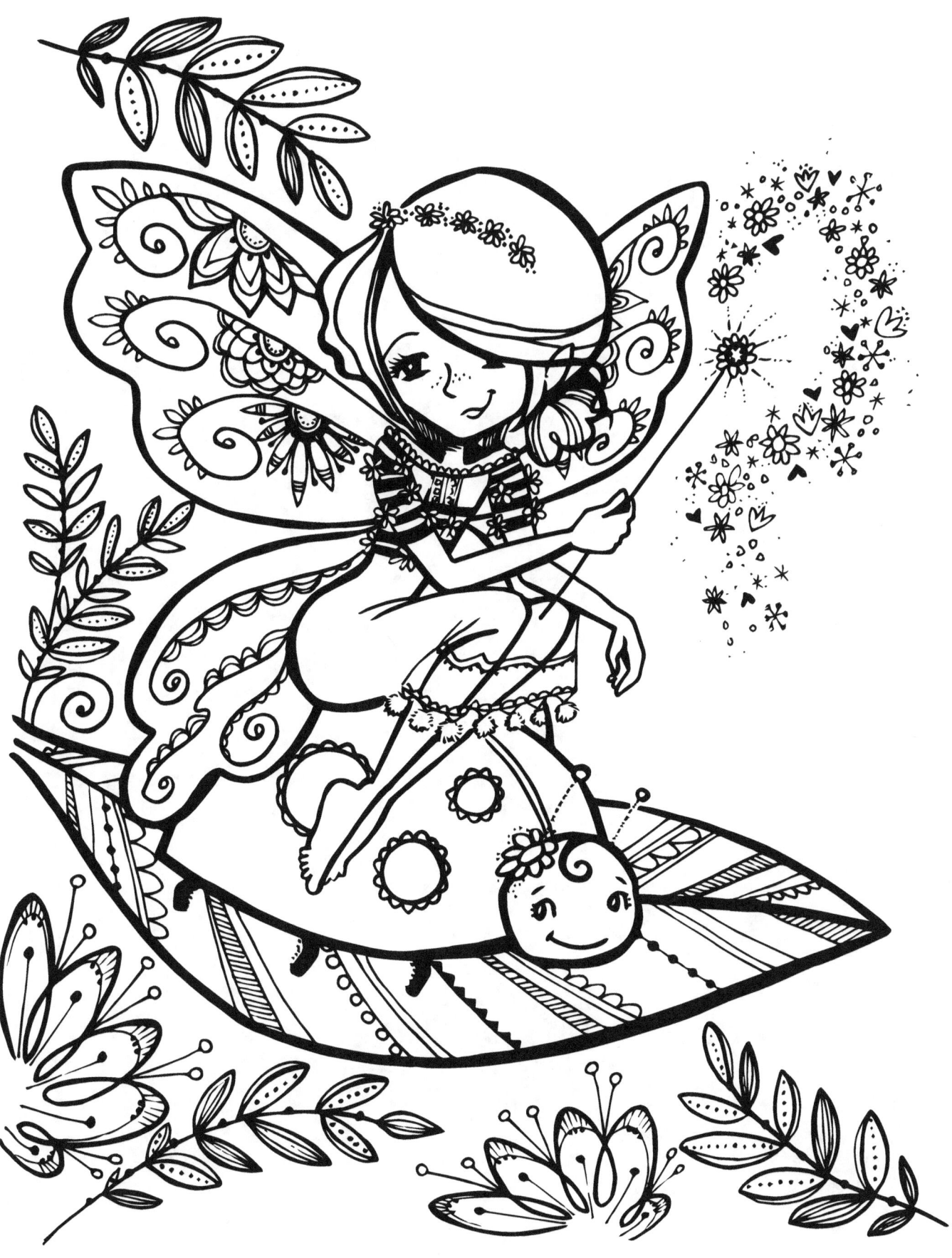

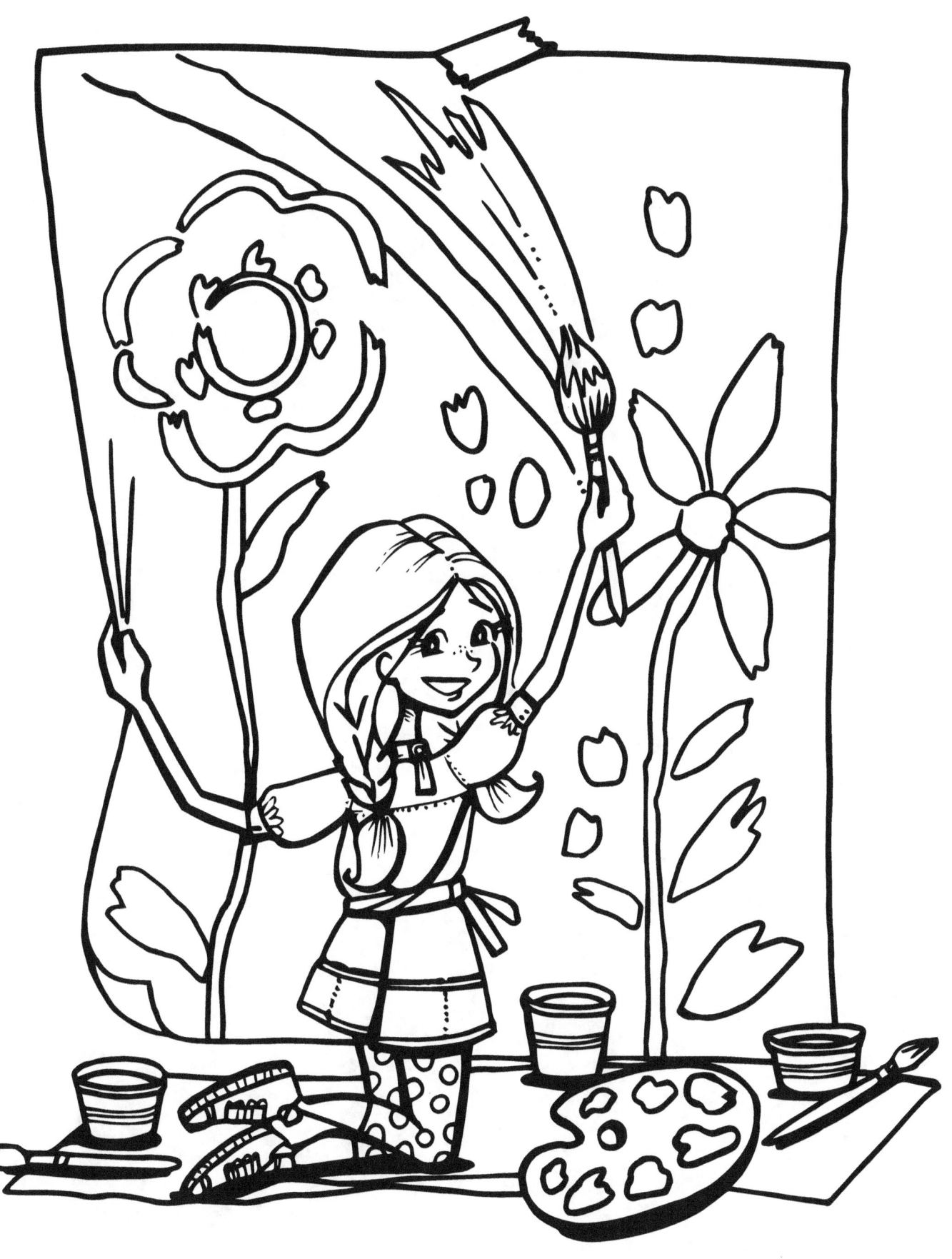

flower girlies

StephAnie Corfee
ARTWORKS

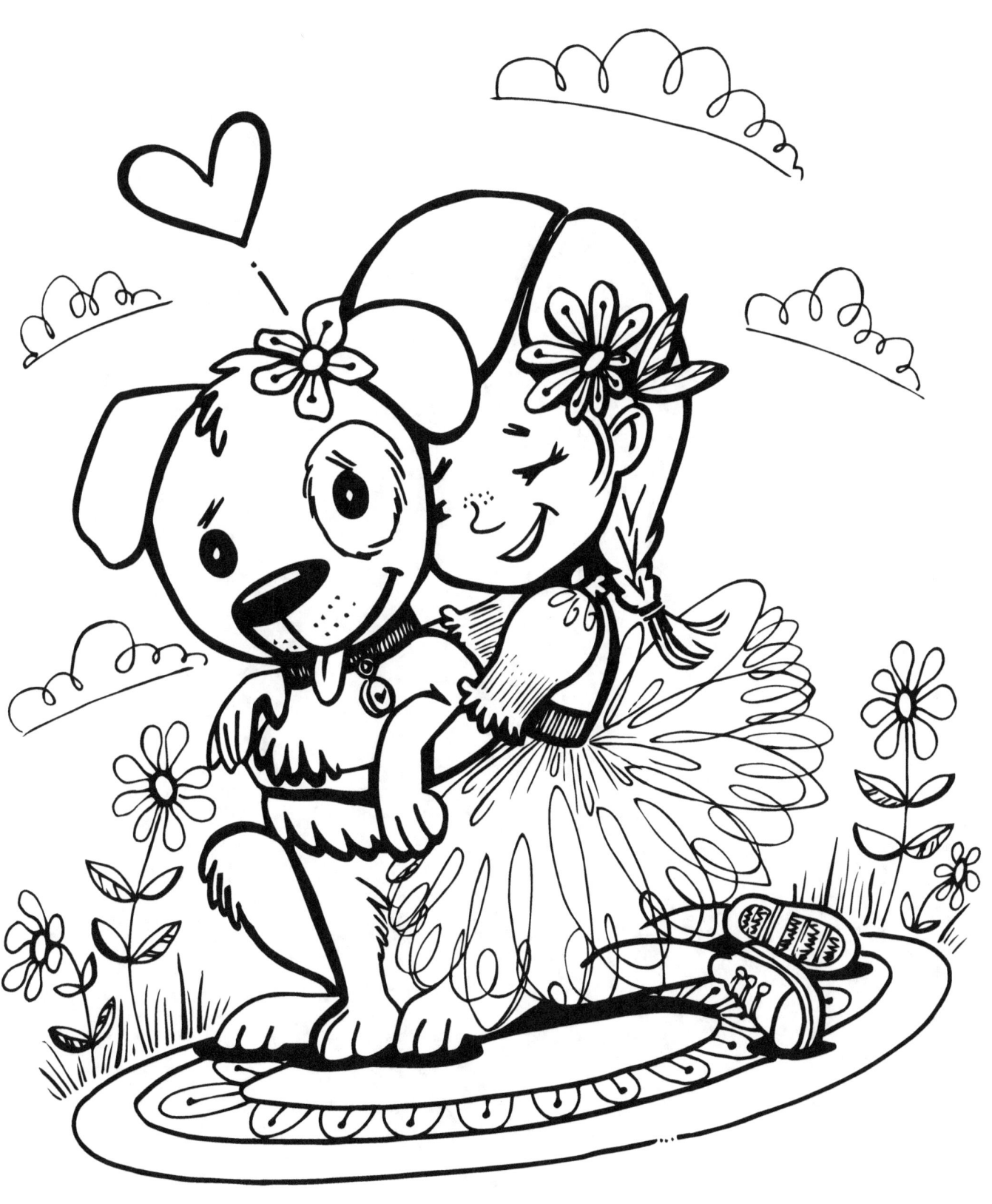

flower girlies

StepHanie Corfee
ARTWORKS

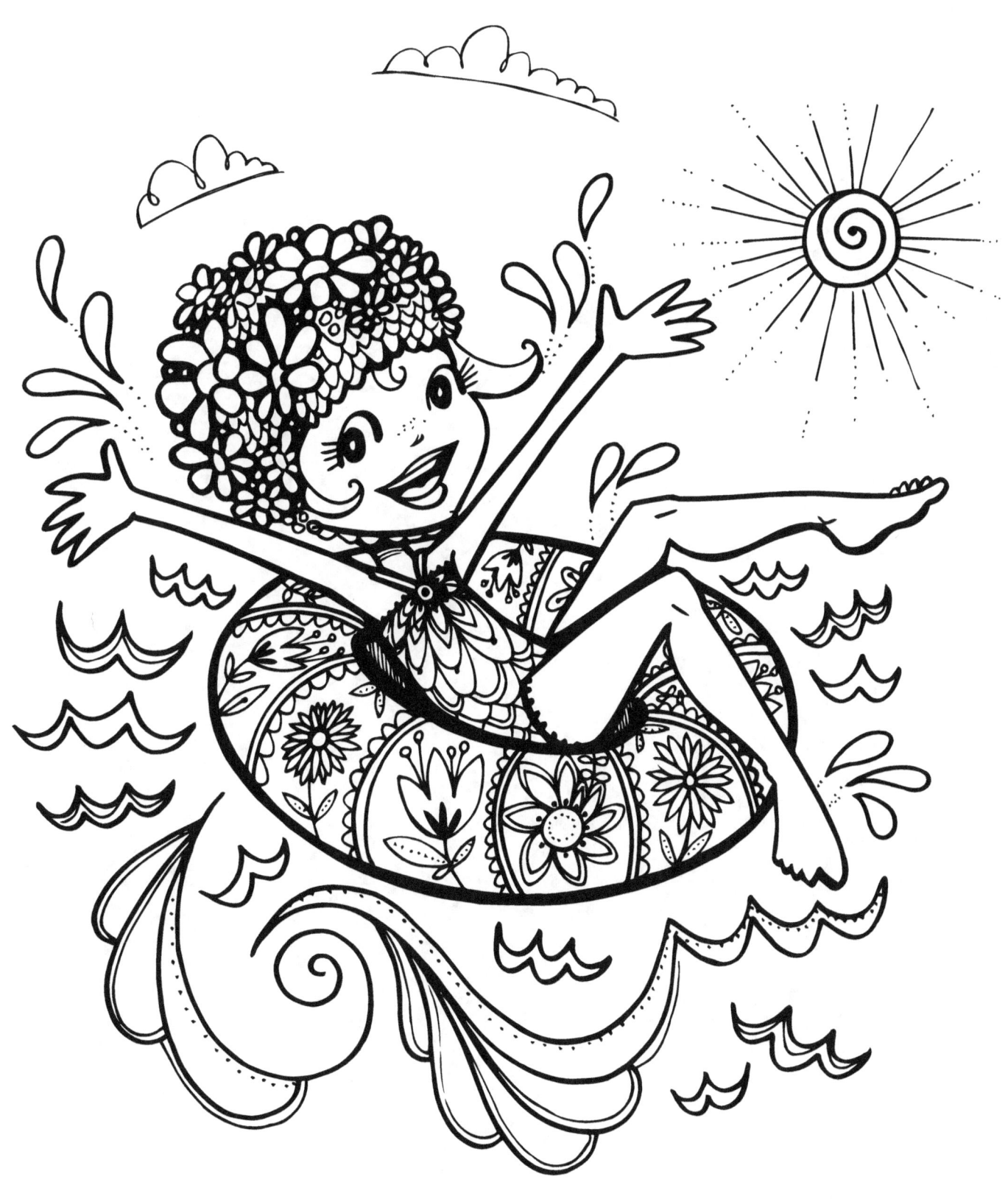

flower girlies

StephanieCorfee
ARTWORKS

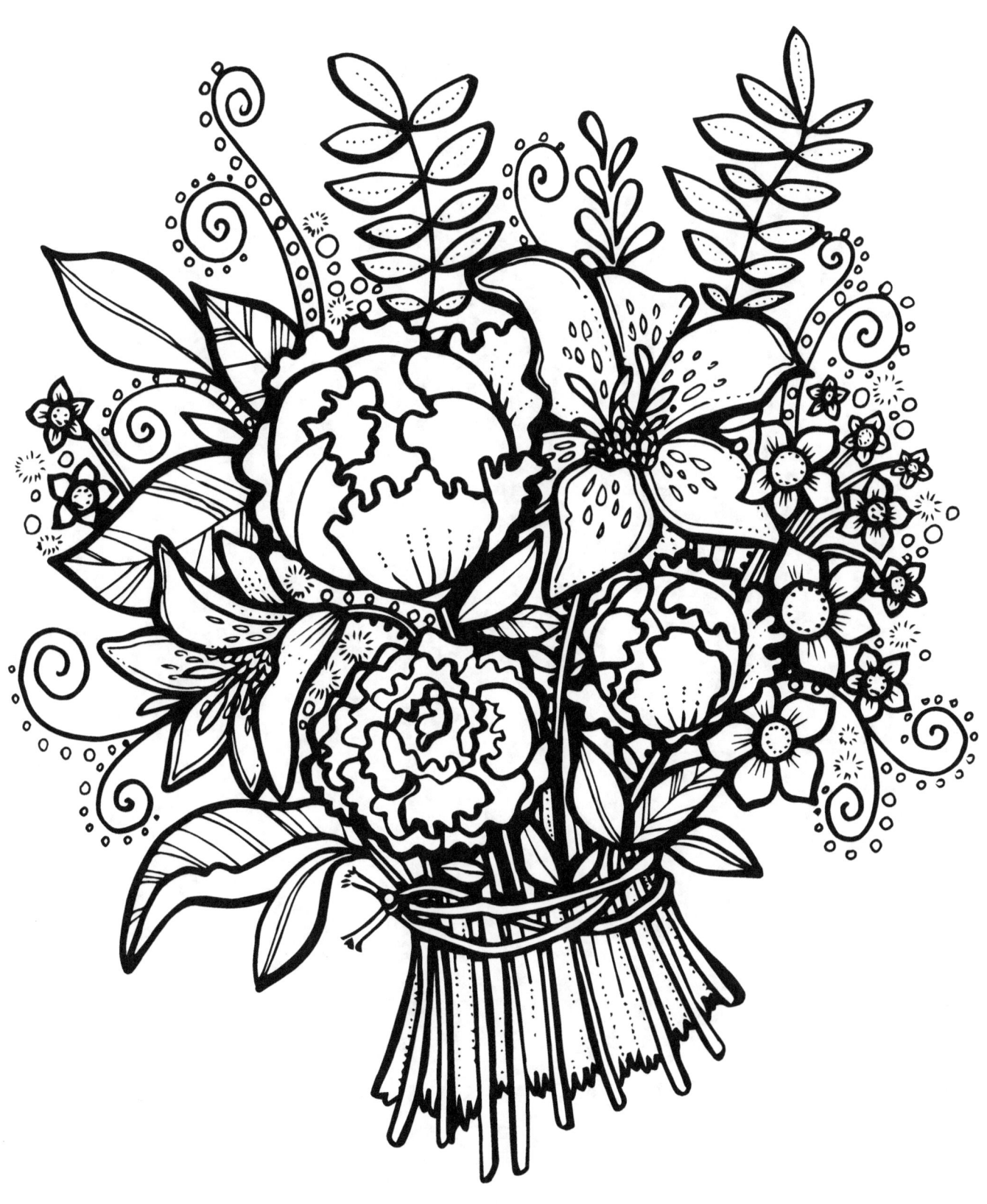

flower girlies

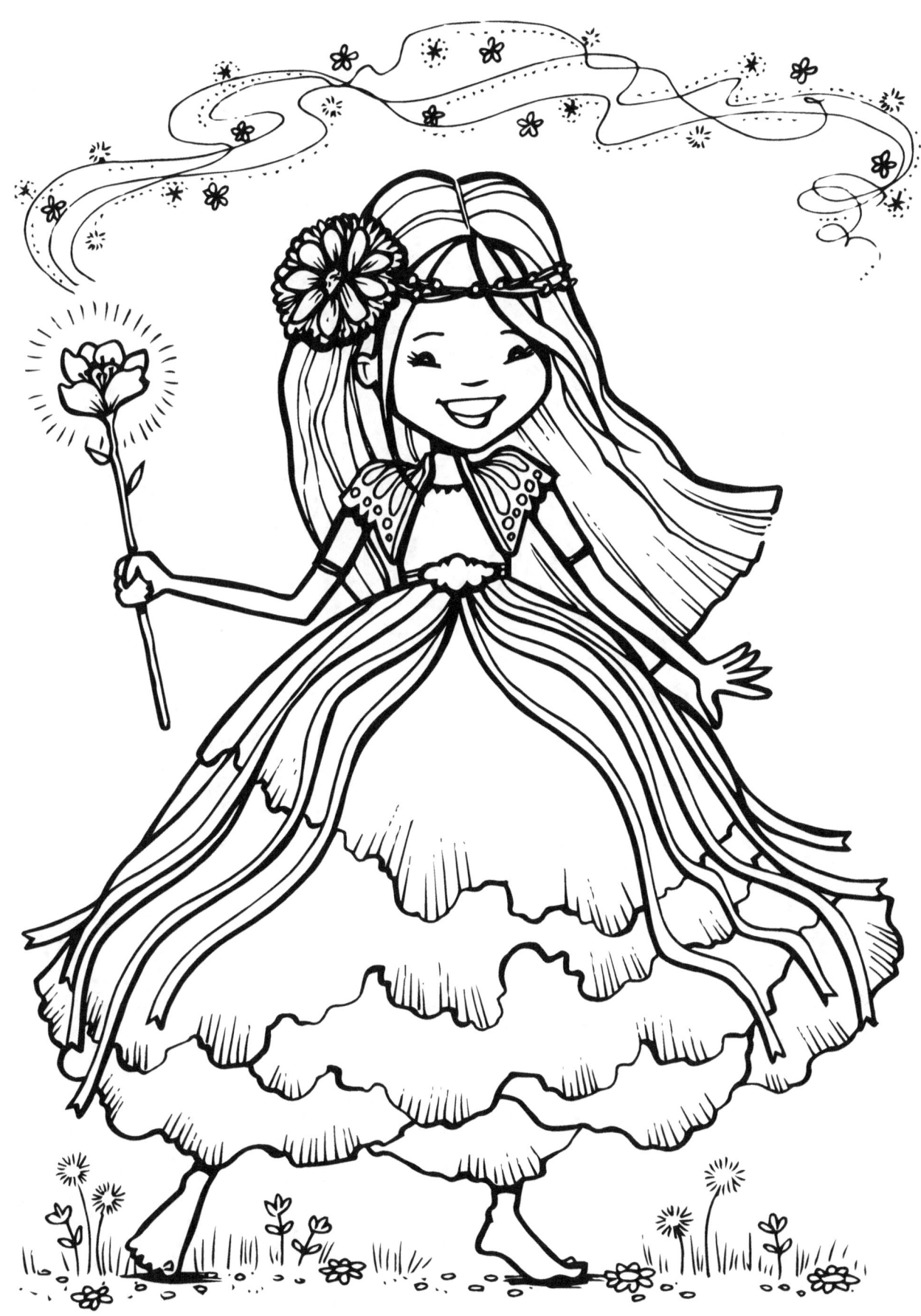

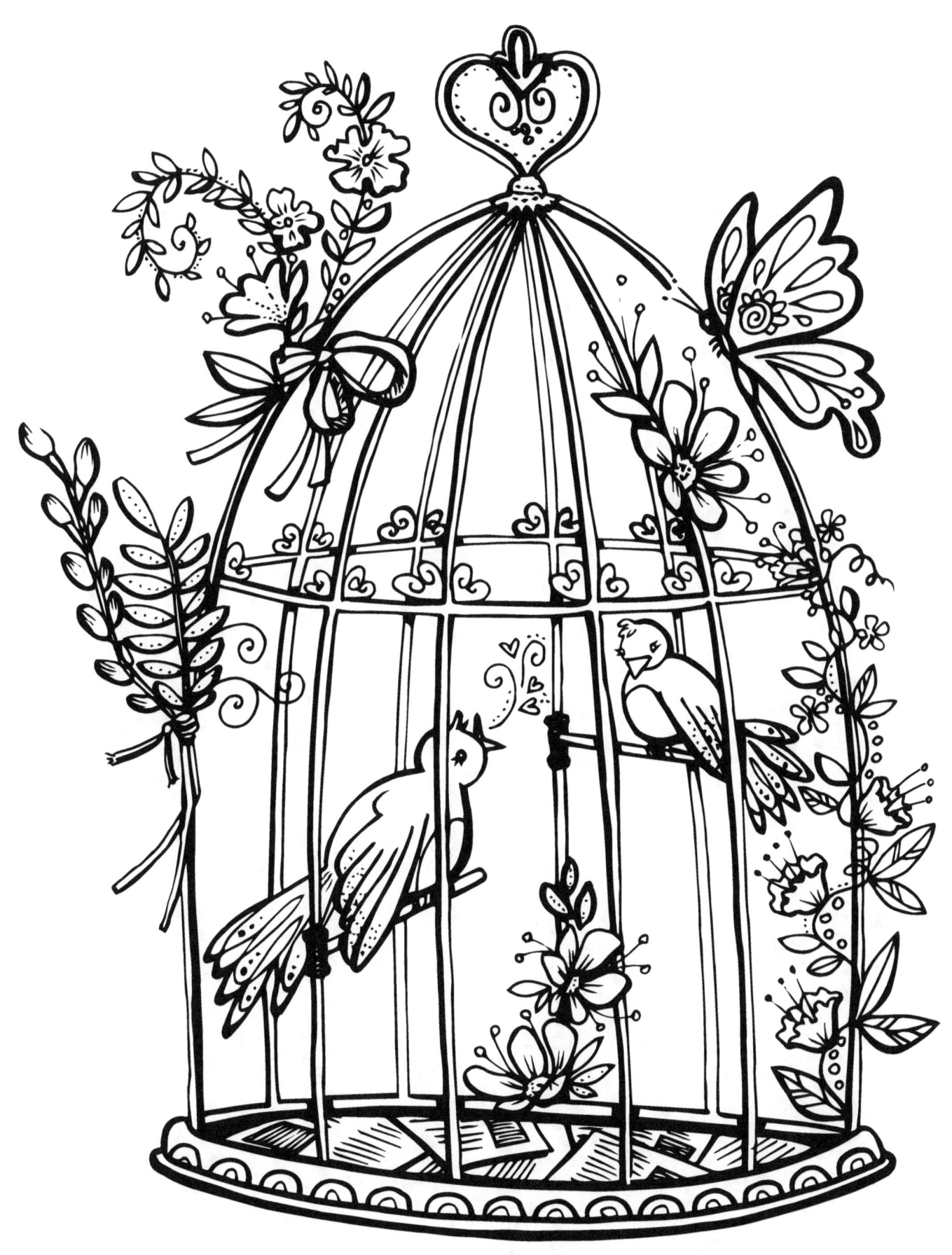

flower girlies

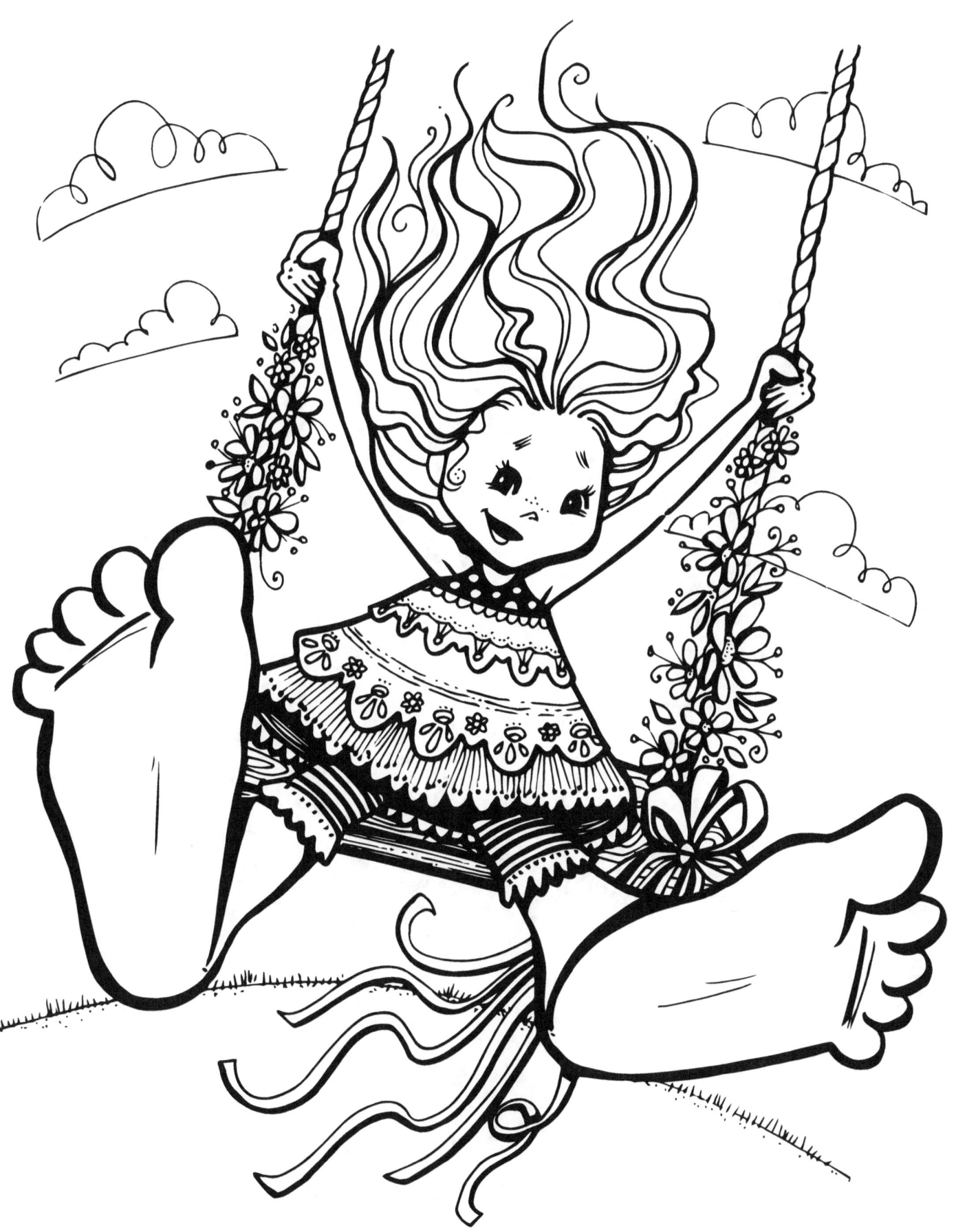

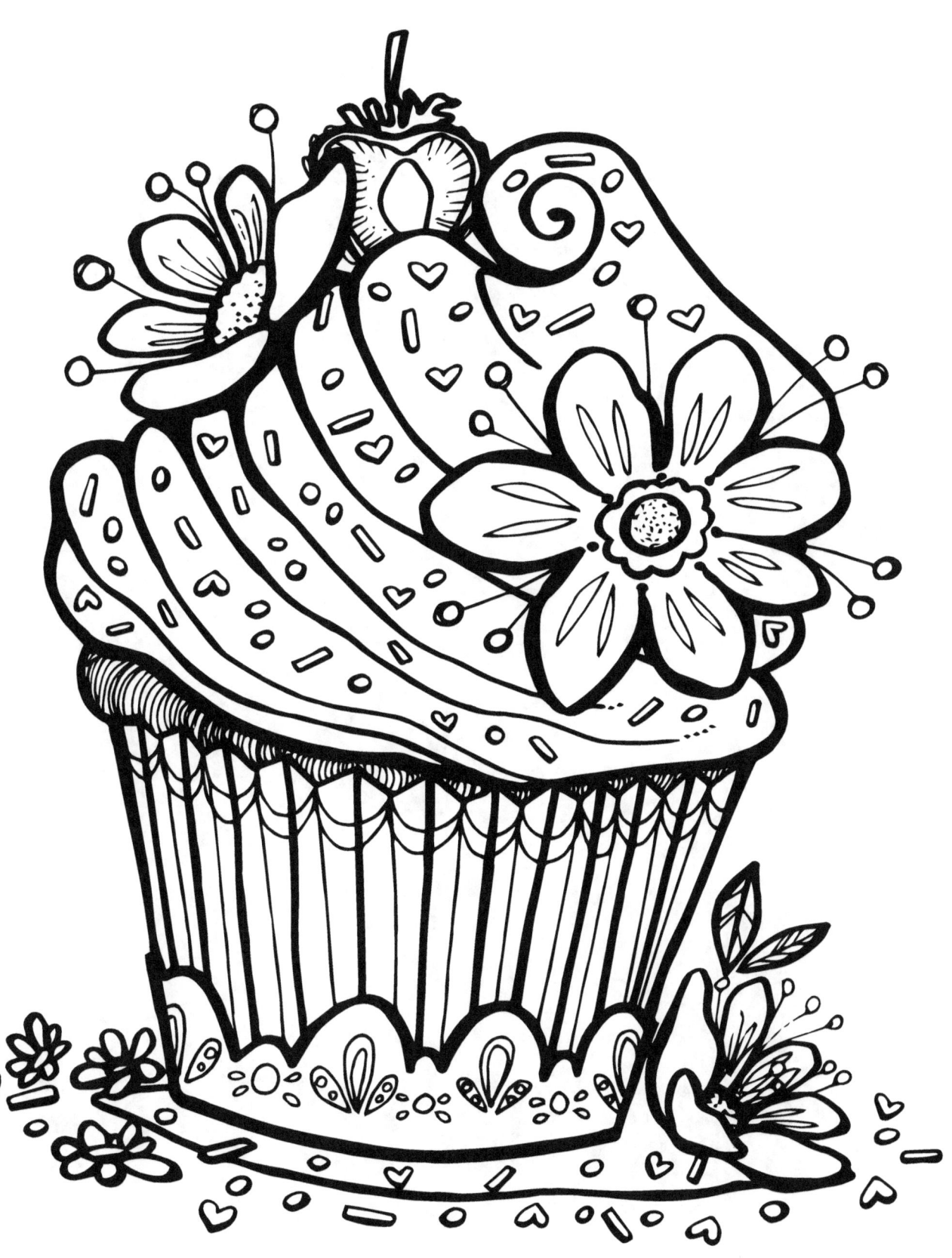

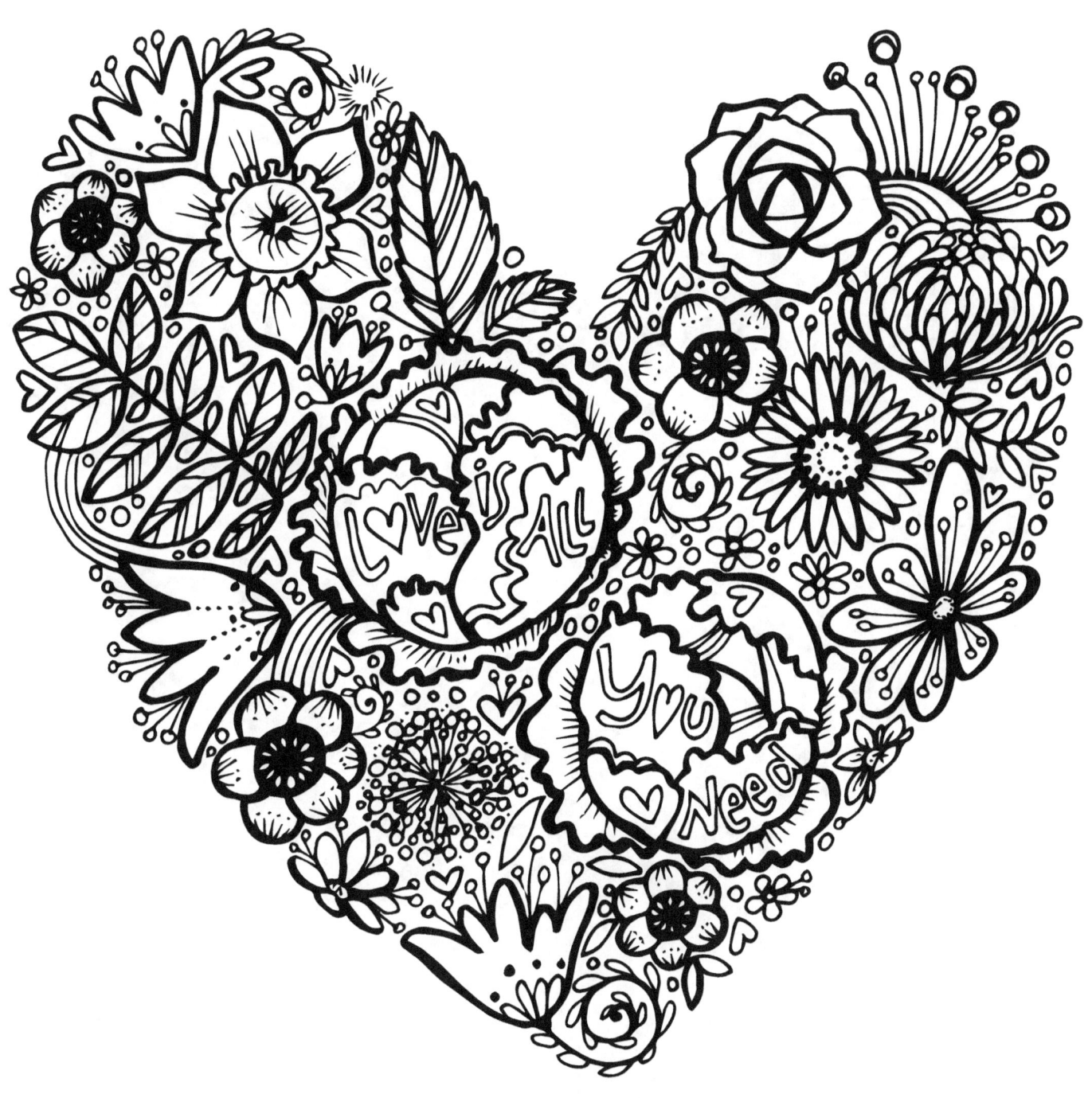

flower girlies

StephanieCorfee
ARTWORKS

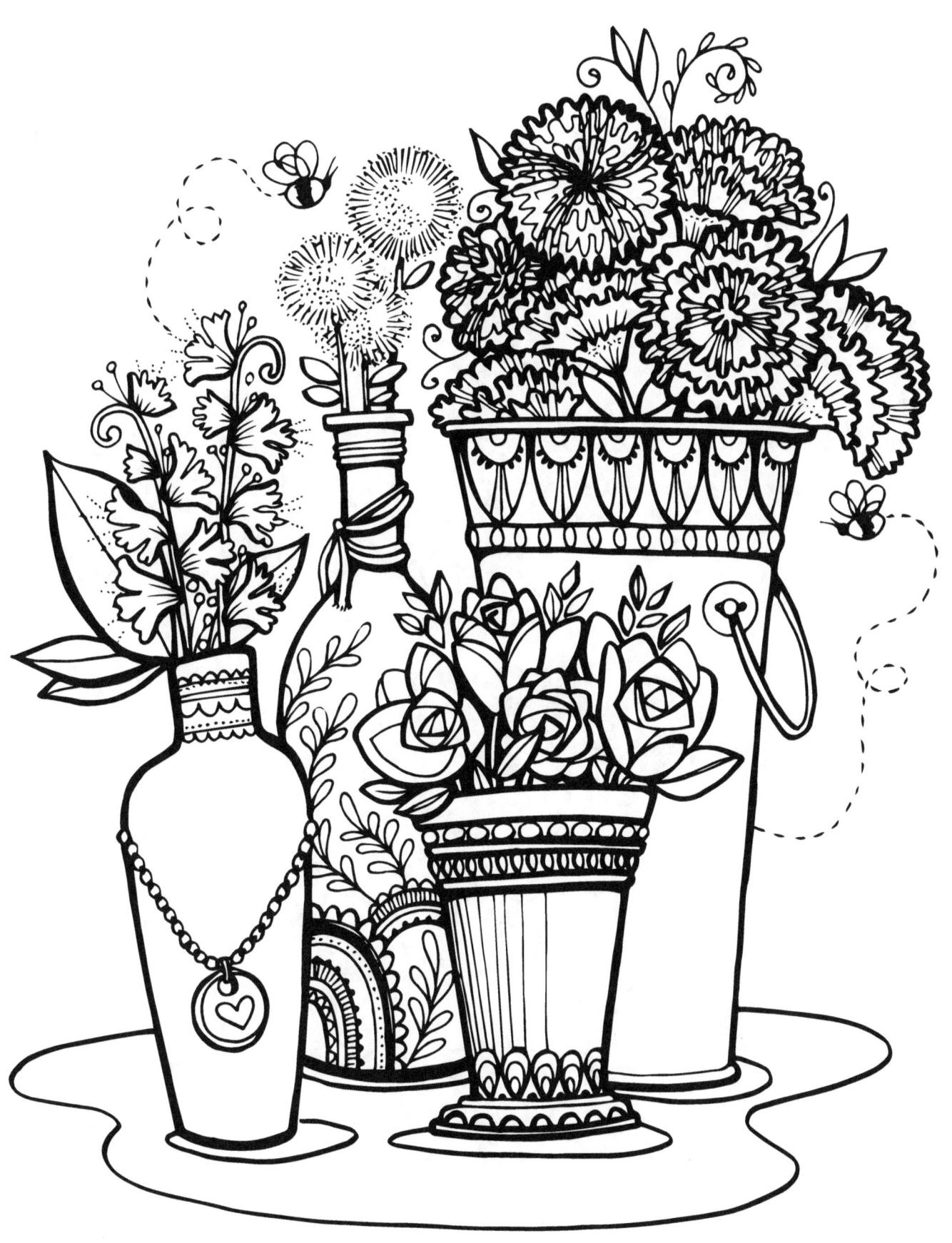

flower girlies

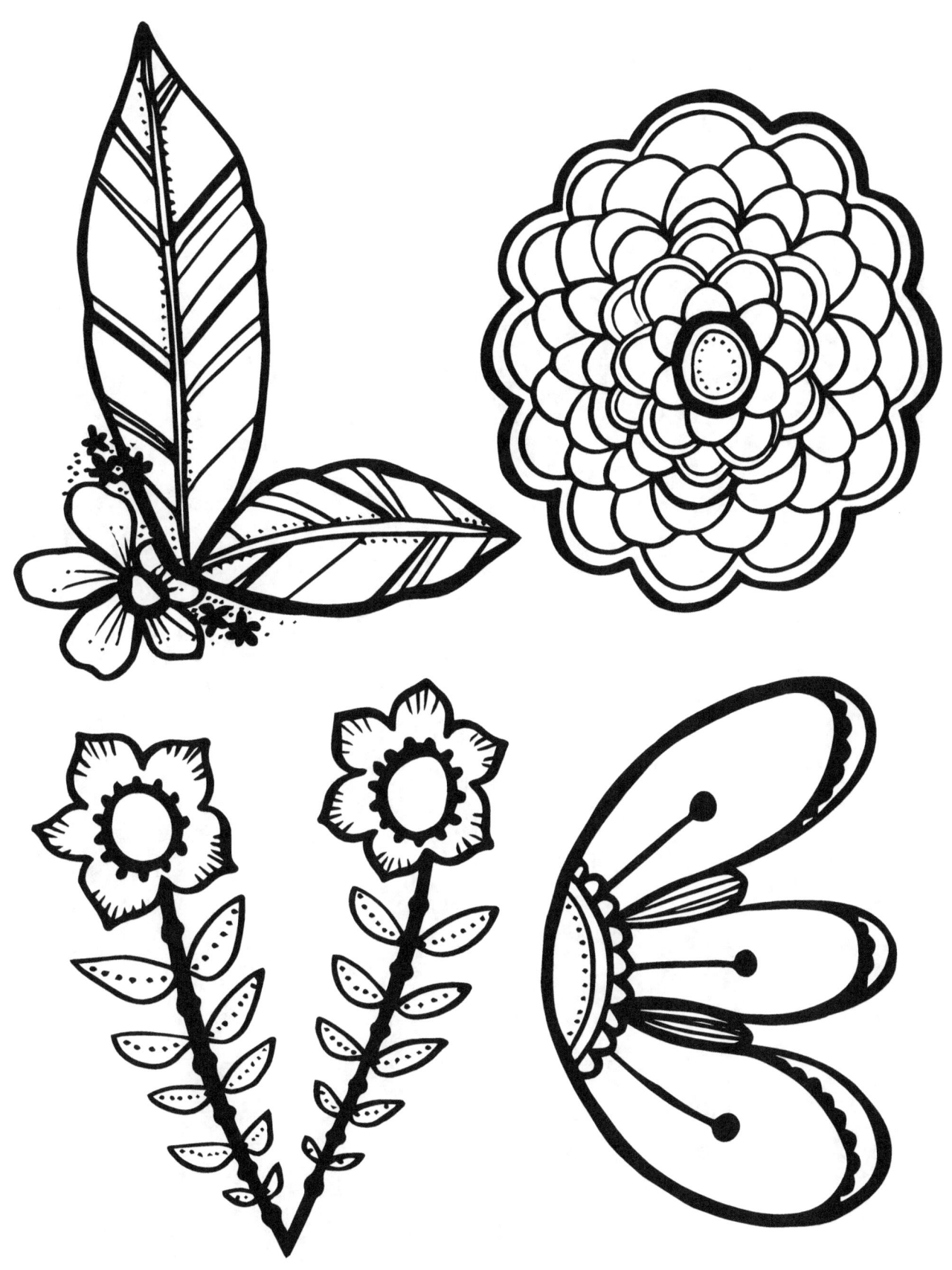

flower girlies

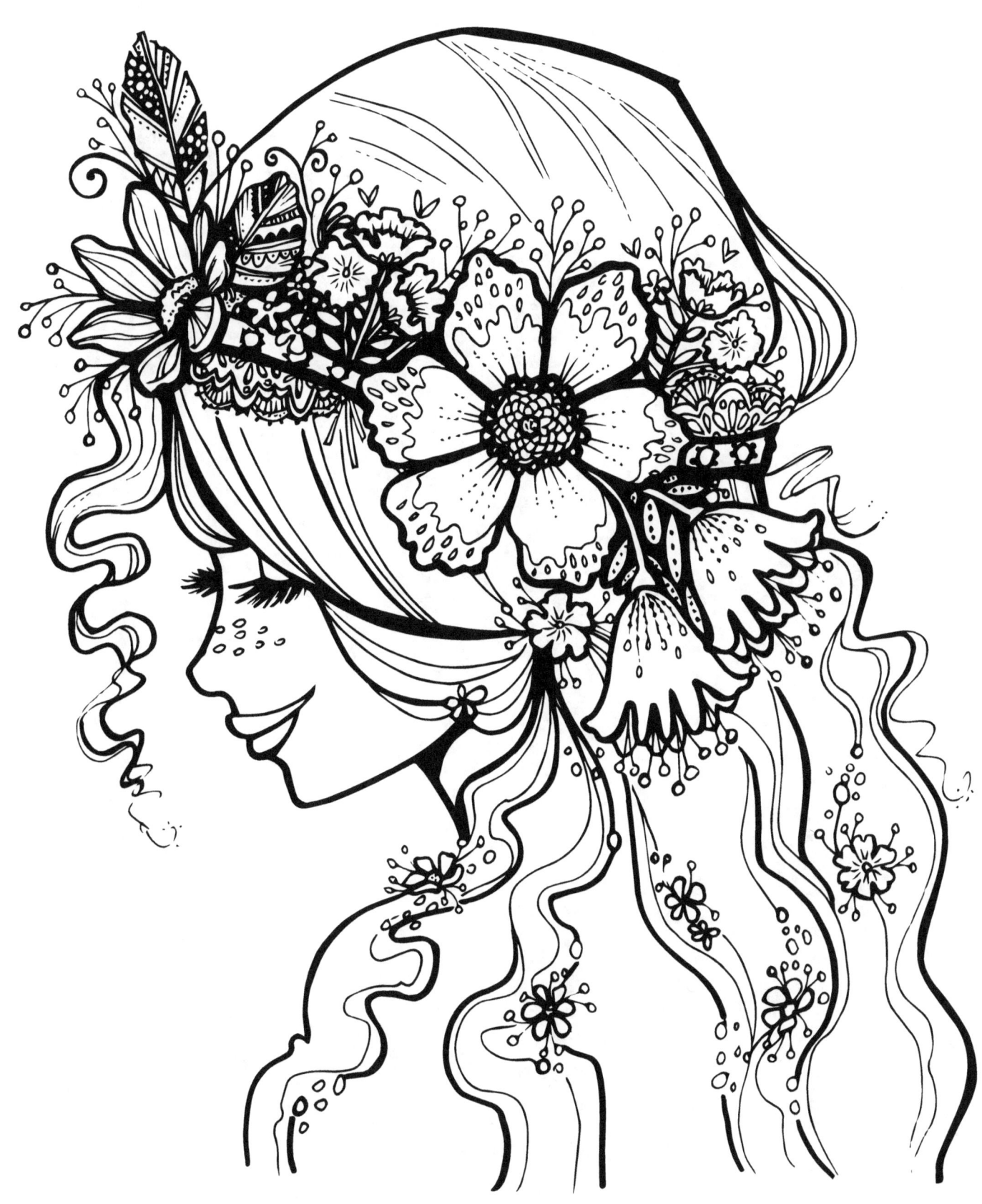

flower girlies

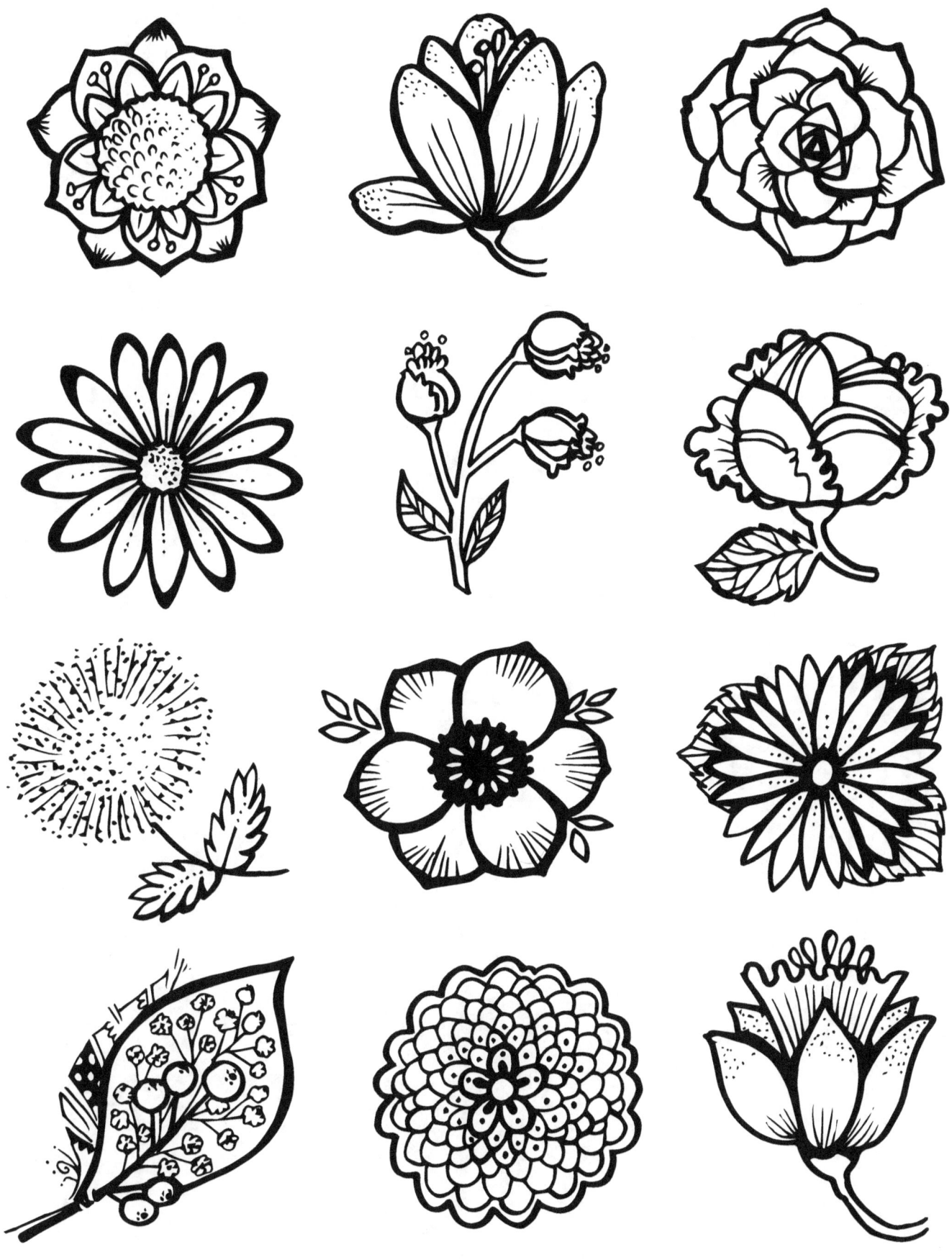

flower girlies

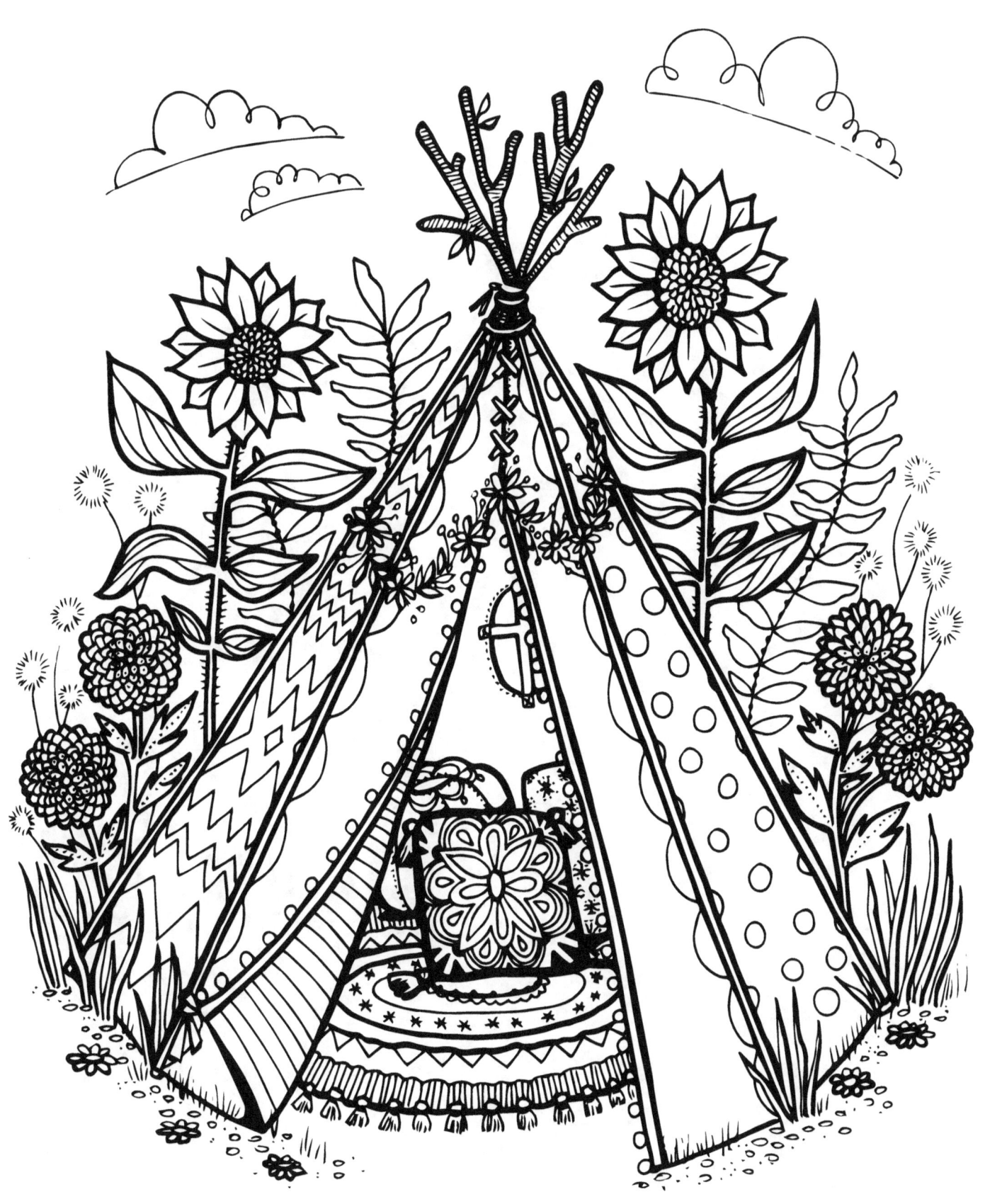

flower girlies

flowers in my Hair

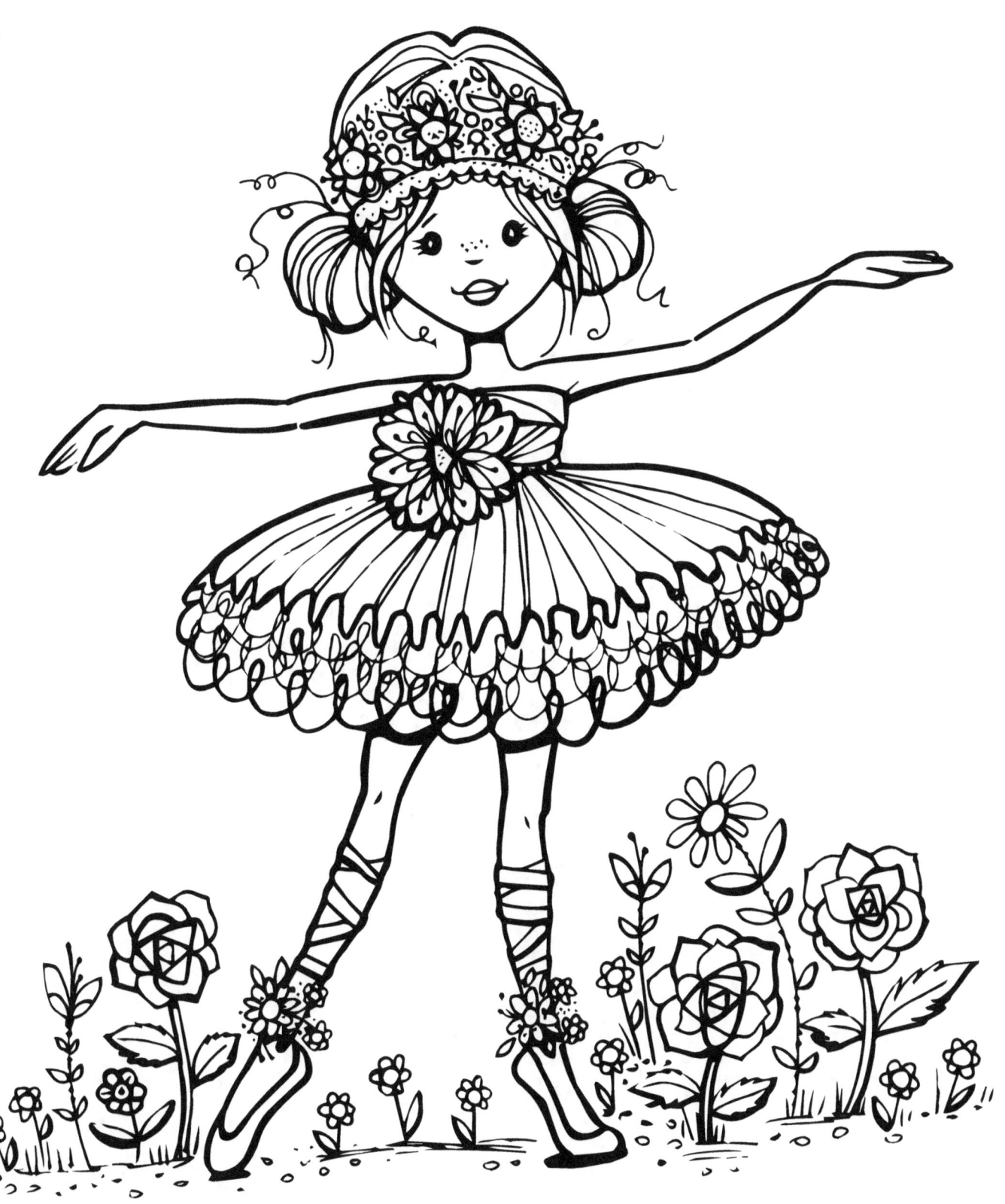

flower girlies

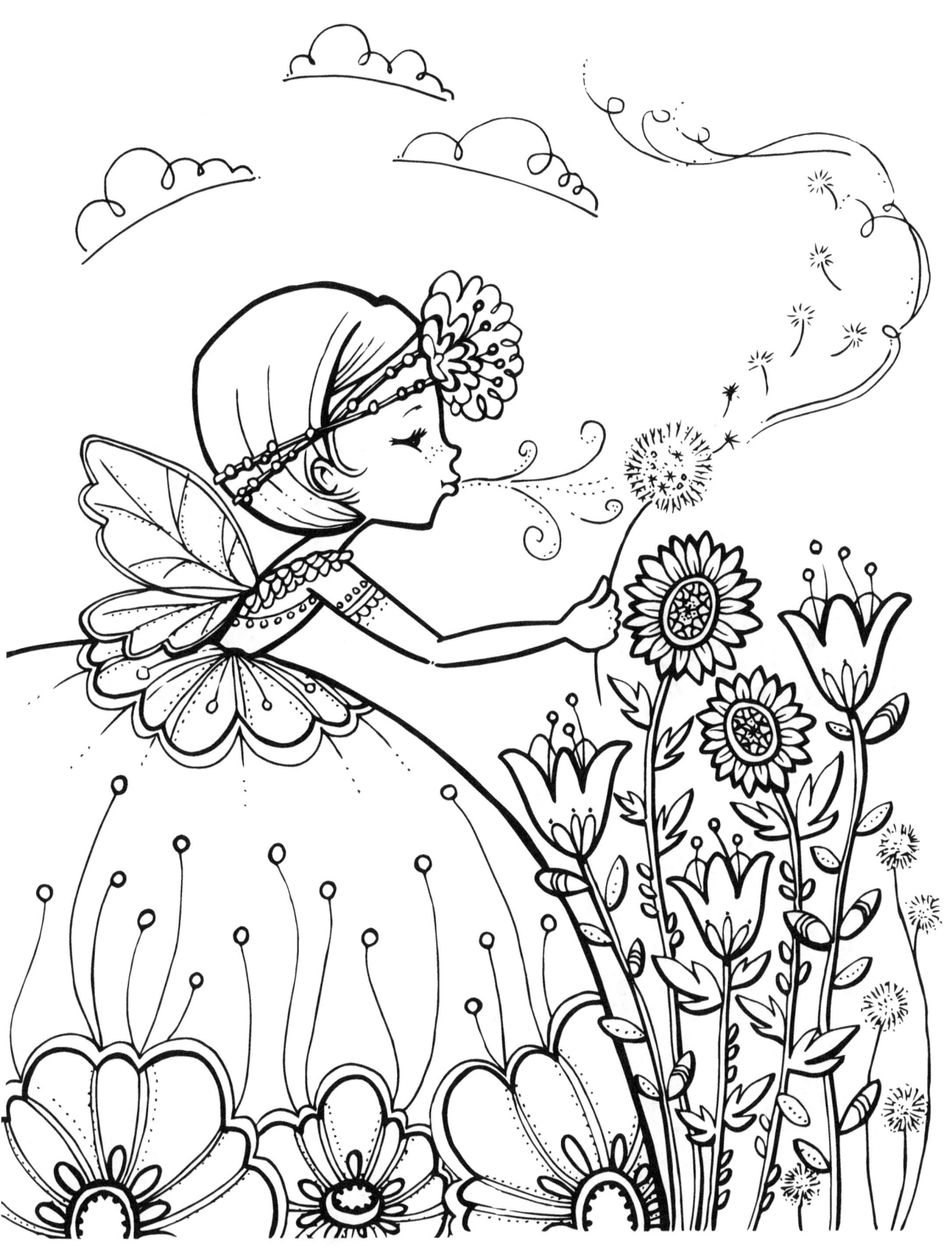

flower girlies

StephanieCorfee
ARTWORKS

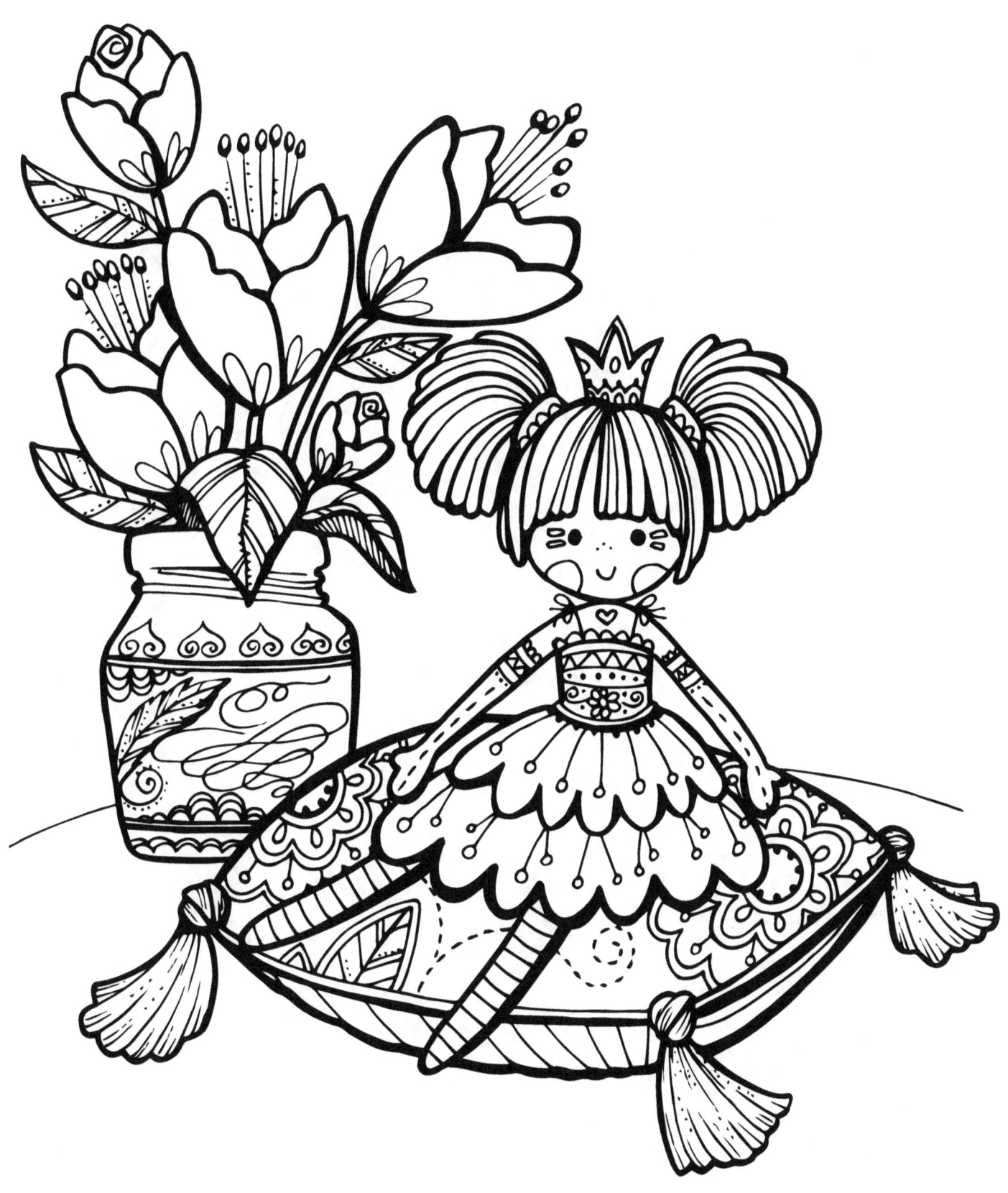

flower girlies

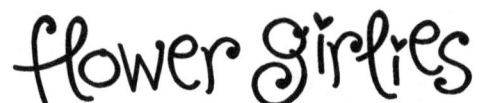

stephaniecorfee.com